THE SOUNDS, FORMS, AND USES OF ITALIAN: AN INTRODUCTION TO ITALIAN LINGUISTICS

Gianrenzo P. Clivio and Marcel Danesi

Here at last is a text on Italian linguistics that clearly presents all of the key concepts in a form designed specifically for English-speaking students. This unique book will fill a major gap in the curriculum of undergraduate and graduate programs in Italian linguistics.

The authors explain complex linguistics ideas in a logical, succinct, and accessible style. Subjects and concepts such as phonetics, phonology, morphology, syntax, semantics, discourse, and variation are treated in detail, using carefully selected examples. The follow-up activities at the end of each chapter provide opportunities for review and practical application, with questions that invite reflection and additional research.

The Sounds, Forms, and Uses of Italian will serve as a basic reference for anyone with an interest in the Italian language. Teachers of Italian at all levels will find it a valuable resource, and students will appreciate the clarity and ease with which it guides them through a difficult subject.

(Toronto Italian Studies)

GIANRENZO P. CLIVIO is Professor, Department of Italian Studies, University of Toronto.

MARCEL DANESI is Director, Semi   Institute, University of Toronto.

The Sounds, Forms, and Uses of Italian: An Introduction to Italian Linguistics

GIANRENZO P. CLIVIO AND MARCEL DANESI

UNIVERSITY OF TORONTO PRESS
Toronto Buffalo London

© University of Toronto Press Incorporated 2000
Toronto Buffalo London
Printed in Canada

ISBN 0-8020-4800-5 (cloth)
ISBN 0-8020-8338-2 (paper)

Printed on acid-free paper

Toronto Italian Studies

Canadian Cataloguing in Publication Data

Clivio, Gianrenzo P.
The sounds, forms, and uses of Italian : an introduction to Italian linguistics

(Toronto Italian Studies)
Includes index.
ISBN 0-8020-4800-5 (bound)   ISBN 0-8020-8338-2 (pbk.)

1. Italian language. I. Danesi, Marcel, 1946– . II. Title. III. Series.

PC1065.C54 2000   450   C00-931429-6

University of Toronto Press acknowledges the financial assistance to its publishing program of the Canada Council for the Arts and the Ontario Arts Council.

University of Toronto Press acknowledges the financial support for its publishing activities of the Government of Canada through the Book Publishing Industry Development Program (BPIDP).

Contents

Preface

A language is the voice of a people, the vocal medium through which the individual members of a culture can express their feelings and thoughts, from the trivial to the sublime, from the witty to the most sombre. The scientific discipline that aims to study this 'voice,' in all its dimensions, is known as *linguistics*.

Among language programs offered by North American universities, Italian figures prominently as a discipline of choice for a large and steadily growing number of undergraduate students. In addition to a broad array of language, literature, and culture classes, many universities and colleges now offer seminars and entire courses in Italian linguistics. However, to the best of our knowledge, appropriate textbooks written in English for the latter – which take into account the students' North American background – are either out of date or virtually impossible to find. Moreover, as instructors of an introductory course in Italian linguistics for nearly three decades at the University of Toronto, we have discovered that the alternative to textbooks written in English, namely those written in Italian and published in Italy, are far too complex for students to follow. The simple reason for this is that their intended users are university students in Italy, not North America. So, over the years, we have taken the path, like many other instructors of Italian linguistics, of preparing and using our own handouts and self-prepared materials. This book constitutes a synthesis of those materials. We sincerely hope that it will fill some of the gap that now exists for the serious study of Italian linguistics in North America.

We must warn the users of this book, however, that the topics chosen for presentation, and the ways in which we have treated them, reflect our own view both of linguistic theory and of how much material a student can handle in an introductory course format. Moreover, in order to keep the proportions of this volume within the limits of a basic textbook, it was necessary to limit the choices to those topics and activities that we have found to be the most useful and practicable in a classroom situation.

Users of This Book

Some knowledge of the Italian language is assumed, although, by working through the textbook, the student will, more than likely, gain a firmer grasp of the language as he or she learns to use the analytical tools that linguistics provides. This book can also be used profitably for self-study, since we believe it can help students strengthen their formal knowledge of the Italian language through the apparatus of linguistic notions and concepts. In the same manner that knowledge of musical theory can help the pianist become a more knowledgeable and proficient performer, so too can skill at linguistic analysis help the language student become more adept at penetrating the internal workings of the language she or he is studying.

We also believe that this textbook can be used as a reference manual, or even as a course book, in programs of general or Romance linguistics. For this reason, we have written it in a generic way, with plenty of Italian examples that we have often glossed in English to facilitate comprehension. Moreover, we have added an Italian–English glossary at the back for easy reference.

Format and Contents

The nine chapters in this book fall into three thematic areas. The first two are introductory in nature: Chapter 1 deals with the origins of the Italian language, and Chapter 2 with the nature of linguistic inquiry and methodology. Chapters 3 to 7 deal with the 'nuts and bolts' of linguistic analysis – phonetics, phonology, morphology, syntax, and semantics. Whereas the chapters on phonetics and phonology have been designed as comprehensive treatments of the subject matter, those on grammar (morphology and syntax) and semantics have been composed necessarily as partial and selective treatments (given the amount of space that would otherwise have been needed). The final two chapters of the book are concerned respectively with discourse and variation (historical and regional).

To render each chapter pedagogically useful, we have used numerous illustrative examples and have added a series of activities (questions and exercises) in a 'Follow-Up' section so that the student can gain practical knowledge of the subject matter and techniques introduced in the chapter.

We have also appended two glossaries at the back of the book: a glossary of technical terms and a glossary of the Italian words used in the nine chapters. Finally, we have provided a brief list of suggested readings for those students interested in getting more detailed information on the various topics treated.

We wish to thank the editorial staff at University of Toronto Press for all their advice, support, and expert help in the making of this textbook. We are especially grateful to Dr Ron Schoeffel and Anne Forte, without whom this volume would never have come to fruition. We also thank the Faculty of Arts and Science of the University of Toronto for having allowed us the privilege of teaching and coordinating the Italian linguistics program of the university. Another debt of gratitude goes to the many students we have taught. Their enthusiasm has made our job as teachers simply wonderful. They are the impetus for this book.

Gianrenzo P. Clivio
Marcel Danesi
University of Toronto, 2000

THE SOUNDS, FORMS, AND USES OF ITALIAN:
AN INTRODUCTION TO ITALIAN LINGUISTICS

1

The Italian Language

As a poet there is only one political duty, and that is to defend one's language against corruption.

W.H. Auden (1907–1973)

The great Romantic English poet Lord Byron (1788–1824) described Italian as a language that sounds 'as if it should be writ on satin.' Byron's description is not an isolated expression of poetic fancy but, in fact, a popular view of the Italian language across the world, often called the language of 'love,' 'poetry,' and 'song.'

To a linguist this is all fine and dandy and, as a layperson, he or she would probably agree that Italian is indeed a melodious language. However, as a hard-nosed scientist, he or she would also be quick to emphasize that the syllabic structure of Italian, and especially the fact that most of its words end in a vowel, are a large part of the reason why the language is perceived by so many people to be mellifluous to the ear. Italian is no more poetic or beautiful than any other language. It is an equal among equals. Perceptions of what is beautiful in a language are just that – perceptions. All languages, no matter what sounds they possess, allow their speakers to express sublime sentiments, as well as to carry out more pedestrian social functions, such as daily communicative exchanges with the other members of their community.

The Italian language is one of a group of languages known as **Romance** languages. It is spoken by about 60 million people in Italy, 23,000 in the Republic of San Marino, 400,000 in Switzerland, another 1.3 million in other European countries, and approximately 6 million in North and South America. Like the other Romance languages, it is the direct offspring of the Latin spoken by the Romans who introduced their language to the peoples under their dominion. Of all the Romance languages, Italian retains the closest resemblance to Latin. The struggle between the written language and the various forms of the living speech, most of which were derived from vulgar Latin, 'the Latin spoken by the common people,' was nowhere so intense or so protracted as it was in Italy.

The purpose of this chapter is to paint a broad historical picture of the Italian language, with a focus on its origins, its uses by well-known writers, and the major features that give it what Lord Byron called its 'satin' quality.

Origins

Italian, French, Spanish, Portuguese, Romanian, Friulian, Sardinian, Rumansh, and a few other languages are all modern-day descendants of the same parent language, Latin. In effect, they are all **dialects** of Latin spoken in territories that achieved nationhood at some point after the demise of the Roman Empire. Their status rose to that of *national languages*, not because they were forged as such, but because they achieved autonomy from the parent language as a result of political, social, and other nonlinguistic factors.

To grasp more concretely the reason why linguists say that the Romance languages are related historically, observe the close affinity that exists in the Italian, French, and Spanish versions of three Latin words:

LATIN	ITALIAN	FRENCH	SPANISH
NOCTE(M) *night*	notte	nuit	noche
OCTO *eight*	otto	huit	ocho
TECTU(M) *roof*	tetto	toit	techo

Now, let us focus more closely on the Latin cluster *ct* (pronounced /kt/), comparing it with its equivalents in the Romance languages. As can be seen from the chart, in Italian, the cluster *ct* corresponds to *tt*, in French to *it*, and in Spanish to *ch* (pronounced more or less like English *ch* in *birch*). These are, in effect, the 'outcomes' of Latin /kt/ in Italian, French, and Spanish:

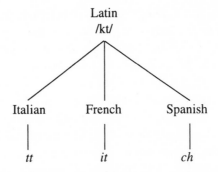

This method of careful comparison has provided us with an initial, albeit tentative, basis for predicting how the /kt/ in such Latin words as *LACTE(M) ('milk') and FACTU(M) ('fact') would probably be pronounced in these three languages. Indeed, even without knowing the actual words for 'milk' and 'fact' in Italian, French, and Spanish, our previous analysis has allowed us to guess intelligently that the Italian word would probably show *tt*, the French word *it*, and the Spanish word *ch*, in place of *ct*. Here are the actual words in these languages:

LATIN	ITALIAN	FRENCH	SPANISH
LACTE(M)	latte	lait	leche
FACTU(M)	fatto	fait	hecho

Clearly, this analytical technique has proved to be extremely useful because it has shown us how certain words are related phonetically to each other and how they have evolved systematically from the same source language. In fact, if we were to continue comparing Italian, French, and Spanish words derived from Latin words containing the cluster /kt/, we would be able to formulate a rule of historical change as follows (the symbol > means 'develops to'):

- /kt/ > /tt/ in Italian
- /kt/ > /i̯t/ in Old French (/i̯/ is a semivocalic sound similar to the *y* in English *say*; but it is no longer pronounced in Modern French)
- /kt/ > /č/ in Spanish (/č/ is a consonant pronounced more or less like the second *ch* in *church*).

Having unravelled this 'historical rule' through a comparative analytical method, we are now ready to go one step further and attempt a phonetic explanation as to how the /kt/ developed into Italian *tt,* French *it,* and Spanish *ch.* In Italian, it can be seen that the Latin /k/ **assimilated** completely to /t/. In Old French, the assimilation was only partial, since the area of articulation of the semi-vowel sound /i̯/ in the mouth is close, but not identical, to that of /t/. This particular type of assimilation is called **vocalization.** In Spanish, the /k/ and /t/ appear to have merged, so to speak, to produce a *palatal* sound, /č/, which is articulated midway between /k/ and /t/. The process is known, logically, as **palatalization.** Comparisons among the three languages in other areas of pronunciation, and in areas of grammar and vocabulary as well, will pinpoint just as precisely how they are related historically. Any form showing a 'deviation' from any established historical rule would then be interpreted either as having been introduced later into the language or as having been subjected to factors interfering in the 'historical process.'

More to the point of this chapter, the above analysis makes it obvious why Italian is defined linguistically as a 'descendant' of Latin and a 'sister' language of the other Romance languages. Many linguists prefer, in fact, to designate the Romance languages as **neo-Latin dialects** instead. From a purely linguistic standpoint, all the 'dialects' spoken in Italy (Sicilian, Calabrese, Venetian, Neapolitan, etc.), Spain (Aragonese, Leonese, etc.), and the other Romance-speaking areas of the world are, in effect, neo-Latin dialects: that is, descendants of Latin.

To be more precise, the Romance languages did not develop directly from classical Latin, but from the colloquial Latin of late Roman times, known as **vulgar Latin,** so called because it was the language spoken by the VULGUS ('the common people'). The forms of this language are reconstructed by linguists on the basis of inscriptions and certain manuscripts that time has preserved:

- An inscription on a wall in Pompeii, for instance, contains the vulgar form ORICLAS instead of the classical AURICULAS ('ears'), thus showing that the AU was being pronounced by the VULGUS as the single vowel *o.*
- In an anonymous appendix to a grammar of Latin by Valerius Probus, a grammarian who is thought to have lived in the first century AD, vulgar spoken forms are compared with the correct classical forms, thus providing, in effect, a treasury of information on how vulgar Latin was spoken (this work is now known generally as the ***Appendix Probi***).

- Many vulgar Latin forms and expressions are also found in the works of various authors, for example, the *Satyricon* by the first-century writer Petronius Arbiter.

Linguists subdivide the Romance languages in various ways, using geographic as well as linguistic criteria. One common geographic method of classification is the following:

- *Insular*: Sardinian (spoken on the island of Sardinia and isolated from other Romance speech at an early date).
- *Continental*: Balkan (Romanian and the extinct Dalmatian language); Western European (Italian, Spanish [including Ladino or Judaeo-Spanish], Portuguese, French, Provençal or Occitan [in southern France], Catalan [in Catalonia and Valencia in Spain, national language of Andorra], and the Rhaeto-Romance group [Romansh, in Switzerland, Ladin and Friulian, in northern Italy]).

Another prevalent method of classifying the neo-Latin tongues is to distinguish between *Western* and *Eastern* languages, with the dividing line being an imaginary one running through La Spezia and Rimini in Italy, called the **Gothic Line** (the dark line drawn on the map on the next page).

The criteria for classifying the Romance languages in this way are purely linguistic. For instance, a characteristic of Western languages that sets them apart from Eastern ones is the **voicing** of the Latin consonants /p/, /t/, and /k/ between vowels. The difference between a *voiced* and a *voiceless* consonant is that in the articulation of voiced consonants the vocal cords in the larynx are made to vibrate, while in the articulation of voiceless consonants they are not. The difference between the voiceless *s* of *sip* and the voiced *z* of *zip* can be easily detected by putting a finger on the larynx while pronouncing each word. In the case of *sip* no vibration will be felt, while in the case of *zip* a distinct vibration can be felt. The /t/ in the Latin word LATU(M) ('side'), for instance, has remained in the Italian form *lato* but has developed into its voiced counterpart in the Spanish form *lado*; the /k/ in URTICA(M) ('nettle grass') has remained in the Italian form *ortica*, but has become voiced in the Spanish form *ortiga*.

Another historical feature that sets Western Romance languages apart from Eastern ones is the **simplification** of double consonants. The double Latin /mm/, for instance, has been simplified to the single

consonant /m/ in Spanish – FLAMMA(M) ('flame') > *llama* – but it has been retained in Italian (*fiamma*), an Eastern Romance language.

A third feature used in the classificatory method is the pluralization process that languages in the two areas undergo. In Western Romance languages nouns are pluralized typically by the addition of a final *-s*: for example, Spanish *libro* ('book') → *libros* ('books') – a process known as the **sigmatic plural** formation. In Eastern Romance languages, on the other hand, nouns are pluralized typically by a change in the final vowel: for example, Italian *libro* → *libri*.

Historical Outline

Pinpointing exactly when a *volgare* (literally, a language 'of the people'), as distinct from Latin, emerged on the Italian peninsula is impossible. The only tools available to the historical linguist are inscriptions and ancient texts containing forms that can be identified as being more 'Italian' than they are 'Latin.' The first text to show a conscious use of the *volgare* is a four-line ninth-century riddle written by a Veronese scribe, and hence called the *Indovinello veronese*. The solution to the riddle is that the scribe is, in effect, writing about himself as someone who, with his pen, is, metaphorically speaking, 'prodding his oxen over white fields' – that is, writing on white paper, 'sowing black seed,' a metaphor for ink:

Se pareva boves	*He prodded his oxen to move forward*
alba pratalia araba	*plowed white fields*
(et) albo versorio teneba	*and a white plow he held*
(et) negro semen seminaba.	*sowing black seed.*

Certain features of this text make it stand out as an early example of the use of a *volgare*:

- The Latin short Ĭ in NĬGRU(M) ('black') is rendered as *e* in *negro*.
- The final Latin U is rendered as *o* in *albo, versorio, negro*.
- The final -T in all the verb forms is missing – *pareba* rather than PAREBAT, *araba* rather than ARABAT, *teneba* instead of TENEBAT, and *seminaba* in place of SEMINABAT.
- The use of *parare* in the sense of 'prodding oxen to move forward' is a meaning that was added to the Latin verb by rustic people.
- The words *versorio* rather than ARATRU(M) and *pratalia* instead of AGROS are lexical features that characterize the Veronese *volgare*.

But it was not the Veronese *volgare* that became the basis of modern-day Italian; rather, it was another *volgare*, spoken in Tuscany, not for any intrinsic linguistic merit it was perceived to have, but because it was the language made famous by three great Tuscan writers – Dante Alighieri (1265–1321), Francesco Petrarca (1304–1374), and Giovanni Boccaccio (1313–1375) in the fourteenth century. Their works became so well known and respected that the *volgare* they used to write their masterpieces of medieval literature came to be known as ***illustre*** ('illustrious'). Gradually, it became the ***lingua letteraria*** ('literary language'), a term that reflected the linguistic reality of Italy until World War II. Up till then the Tuscan-based form of Italian was a language that literate people read and studied, but which few spoke, unless of course they were Tuscan. The language spoken by others in their homes and in the streets was the local *volgare*. All such *volgari* eventually took on the designation of dialects, in the common sense of the word. But it must not be forgotten that all the Italian dialects, including Tuscan, were all at one time rival descendants of the same language, vulgar Latin. Tuscan had the good fortune of having been spoken by three great writers who used their indigenous linguistic competence to write some of the greatest literature of all time.

Adding to the prestige of the Tuscan *volgare* during the fourteenth century was the central position of Tuscany in Italy, and the aggressive commerce of its most important city, Florence. However, it was always literary, rather than purely economic or political, factors that were the primary shapers of the **questione della lingua** throughout the evolution of standard Italian. Before the 1200s the 'literary language' of Italy was Latin. The earliest poetry written in *volgare* was connected with the German Hohenstaufen court, which ruled from Sicily. In the late 1200s the innovations of Guido Guinizelli of Bologna, creator of the **dolce stil nuovo** ('sweet new style'), profoundly influenced Italian writing and, thus, the use of the *volgare*. In this style, the poet dealt with a Platonic love relationship, in which the loveliness of the adored woman removed all carnal desire from the lover. Dante wrote his earliest works in this style. The thirteenth century also produced folk poetry, doctrinal poetry, imitations of the *chansons de geste* in various dialects, and a magnificent flowering of religious poetry in the *laudi* of Jacopone da Todi and in the *Hymn to Created Things* of St Francis of Assisi. *Laudi* in dialogue form represent the beginning of dramatic literature, the *sacre rappresentazioni*. Prose works included translations from the Latin and French as well as collections of tales, anecdotes, and witty sayings.

Especially critical in getting the Tuscan *volgare* into communal consciousness, and thus into wider circulation as a kind of common tongue, was the fact that the works of Dante, Petrarca, and Boccaccio became known widely outside of Italy. Dante's epic masterpiece, *La divina commedia (The Divine Comedy)*, which he probably began around 1307 and completed shortly before his death, showed once and for all that a *volgare* could be used, instead of Latin, to express the noblest of sentiments, the most profound of thoughts. The *Commedia* became an overnight success, so to speak. In the centuries following the invention of printing, almost 400 editions were published. Some of these have even appeared illustrated by Italian masters, such as Botticelli and Michelangelo, and by the English artist William Blake. Boccaccio, too, gained an international public for his *Decameron*. From his psychologically realistic *novelle* were drawn various plots and characters by writers in other countries. In the fifteenth century, however, several influential humanist writers and philosophers, such as Coluccio Salutati, Lorenzo Valla, Marsilio Ficino, and Giovanni Pico della Mirandola, incredibly, sought to reinstate Latin as the literary language. But their reactionary efforts met with little success. By the end of the century the Tuscan *volgare* had firmly embedded itself as the literary language of Italy, never again to be replaced by Latin.

During the Renaissance in the sixteenth century, Italian, as distinct from Latin, became a medium for all kinds of literary expression. Pietro Bembo, who exercised tremendous influence in literary circles, contributed greatly to this development. His *Prose della volgar lingua* established the principle of linguistic purism for Italian literature. Other influential writers of this period were the statesman and political philosopher Niccolò Machiavelli and the poets Lodovico Ariosto, Torquato Tasso, Luigi Pulci, and Matteo Maria Boiardo, who made the Tuscan *volgare* even more popular. The great masterpieces of the period were, undoubtedly, Ariosto's *Orlando furioso* (1516), in which he tells of the varied and improbable adventures of Orlando, and Tasso's *Gerusalemme liberata* (1581), which showed, once and for all, that the *volgare* could express poetic sentiments that reflected all the Aristotelian canons of unity. Other prominent writers of the period were Angelo Poliziano, Michelangelo, Gaspara Stampa, Pietro Aretino, Baldassare Castiglione, and Leon Battista Alberti.

The predominant artistic style of the 1600s was a form of writing characterized by exuberant and often sombre emotion, called *marinismo* (after the poet Giambattista Marino). The poetry in particular was designed to dazzle the reader through an opulent use of rhetorical devices. Toward the end of the century a movement arose in opposition to this so-called 'baroque style,' principally among members of the **Arcadia**, a society founded in Rome in 1690 that advocated a conscious return to simple, straightforward modes of literary expression. The influence of the Arcadia is discernible in the comedies of Carlo Goldoni, one of the great playwrights of Italian literature, who rendered situations simply and forcefully while depicting realistically the milieu from which his characters derived their distinctive qualities. Some Arcadians, notably Pietro Metastasio, also wanted to restore classical restraint to poetry and drama.

The eighteenth century produced major works of journalism by Gaspare Gozzi and Giuseppe Baretti, and of remarkable philosophical and historical erudition, especially by the Neapolitan Giambattista Vico. In that century, the Italian language came under strong influence from outside, namely from French philosophers and writers of the Age of Enlightenment. Words, phrases, and even grammatical constructions were imported into the Italian language and used consciously by writers to exhibit a 'world savvy.' The playwright Vittorio Alfieri and the poet Giuseppe Parini reacted vigorously and effectively against the excessive foreign influences of the era, striving to arouse a sense of national pride and unity against foreign domination by stressing the virtues of *la lingua di Dante*.

From the beginning of the 1800s until 1870, when the removal of French troops from Rome eliminated the last trace of foreign domination, the prevailing influences on the Italian language and literature were Romanticism and nationalism, as is directly evident in the writings of the political thinker Giuseppe Mazzini and in the work of such poets as Ugo Foscolo and especially Giacomo Leopardi, who stands out as one of the greatest lyric poets in Italian literature. Nationalism gave rise to three strains in nineteenth-century Italian literature. One was a feeling that themes dealing with real, everyday life were worthy of artistic treatment; the second was the debate that arose on the secular power of the papacy; and the third was a nostalgia for the past. In the second half of the 1800s, writers started to react against the latter trend, advocating everyday speech and a simple style. The movement they initiated came to be called *verismo* ('realism'). The one great novelist of this movement was Giovanni Verga (a leader of the Sicilian realists). Opposed to and yet influenced by the verist trend was the poet Giovanni Pascoli.

A distinguishing feature of Italian Romantic writers was their political involvement in the struggle for Italian independence, known as the *Risorgimento*. The more nationalist or revolutionary writers expressed antagonism to the Church; other writers withdrew to what they considered the more serene values of classical civilization; still others reaffirmed the Christian faith. Alessandro Manzoni, for instance, wrote of the need for a simple, pure language based on the original Florentine model of Dante. Toward the middle of the 1800s the influence of Manzoni and Romanticism in general provoked a reaction accompanied by an aggressive new form of classicism, culminating in the work of the poet Giosuè Carducci, who, incidentally, was awarded the Nobel Prize in 1906 for his efforts.

Writers continued to shape the forms and stylistic features of the Italian language during the first half of the twentieth century. The first writer of influence at the threshold of the century was Gabriele D'Annunzio, who continued to stress the rhetoric and lyricism of Romantic poetry. Movements rose quickly against the Romantic legacy, the most effective and extremist of which was *futurism* – a movement that advocated a simplification of writing style. The founder of futurism, the poet Filippo Tommaso Marinetti, used language stripped to its essentials. At the same time, the philosopher, statesman, literary critic, and historian Benedetto Croce stimulated a nostalgic return to the emotional sentiments and intricate style of Romantic writers, stressing the use of poetic language. In his bimonthly periodical *La Critica*, and in his literary and philosophical works, Croce emphasized the importance of intuition in art and of freedom in the development of civilization. Two other periodicals were established to provide a forum for different groups of Italian writers: *Voce*, which helped modernize Italian culture and introduced into Italy significant French, British, and American ideas; and *Ronda*, a reactionary voice emphasizing a return to classical forms of writing.

A unique figure throughout the first three decades of the century was the novelist, short-story writer, and playwright Luigi Pirandello, who was awarded the Nobel Prize in 1934. Pirandello introduced original dramatic devices into his plays that brought actors and the audience into closer relation. After World War II, a number of Italian writers came into international prominence: Giuseppe Ungaretti, Salvatore Quasimodo, and Eugenio Montale ranked among the foremost European poets of that era. Quasimodo was awarded the Nobel Prize for literature in 1959, and Montale in 1975. A few years after World War II, critics began to speak of an Italian literary **neorealism**. Among the outstanding figures of this movement were the novelists Carlo Levi and Alberto Moravia – the latter a prolific author noted for his novels and short stories dealing with the contemporary, alienated human psyche. Those novelists wrote in a spare, realistic prose style about the moral dilemmas of men and women trapped in banal and boring social and emotional circumstances. Among the more notable postwar novelists are Elsa Morante, whose fiction has an epic, mythic quality, and Natalia Ginzburg, a poet and novelist, renowned for her sensitive, spare treatment of Italian children and women isolated within the family setting.

But in the period after World War II the greatest influence on the development of language in Italy came not from the pen, but from the 'tube.' Until the advent of mass electronic media, and especially television and cinema, writing was the medium through which a 'standardization' of the original Tuscan *volgare* took shape. Italian remained, by and large, a *literary language*, a language studied in schools and read in the print medium. At home and in the streets people spoke their native dialect or a regional variant of the literary language. But with the advent of mandatory schooling and literacy programs after the war, combined with the spread of electronic media throughout the country, virtually everyone in the country was exposed to the same language on a daily, routine basis. No wonder, then, that the process of standardization gained momentum in the 1950s. Television and cinema brought about a radical change in society, replacing the print medium as the primary form of exposing people to the standard language. From the middle part of the twentieth century to the present day there is no doubt that the electronic media have taken over print's historical role in shaping language usage. By the early 1970s, people across Italy were tuning in every day to watch TV programs, whether or not they were literate. The language they heard became part of their system of everyday speech. Today, television has created its own form of literacy that promotes linguistic innovation at a rate that has never been paralleled before in the history of the Italian language.

Dialects

The gist of the foregoing discussion has been that standard Italian, as it is now called, started out as a simple *volgare* spoken in Tuscany, especially in Florence. Throughout the peninsula, other *volgari* had developed from spoken Latin, most with their own oral and literary traditions. As the Tuscan *volgare* was elevated to a literary code, the other *volgari* came to be seen as variants of the language. It was only near the end of the nineteenth century that linguists became interested in classifying the dialects in a systematic fashion, dividing them into several broad areas:

- The Gallo-Italic dialects in the north and northwest: Piedmontese, Lombard, Ligurian, Emilian, and Romagnol, all of which are Western Romance dialects displaying a close affinity to French in their pronunciation.
- The Venetian dialect, which is spoken also in the Italian Tirol and parts of what used to be Dalmatia and Istria, in addition to the Venetian area itself.
- The central dialects, including Tuscan, Corsican, north Sardinian, Roman, Umbrian, and Marchesan.
- The southern dialects: Campanian, Abruzzian, Apulian, Neapolitan, Sicilian, Calabrian, and Lucanian.

The central and southern Sardinian dialects are so distinct from this entire group of dialects that they are classified as a separate branch of the Romance languages, as is Friulian, which is spoken in northeastern Venetia, considered by most linguists to be a Rhaeto-Romansh dialect. In actual fact, within the major dialect areas and subareas are numerous local dialects that vary in pronunciation and vocabulary almost from town to town, from village to village.

The specific linguistic features that separate the major dialects can be pinpointed rather accurately by comparing their forms with their Latin sources. Take, for example, the outcome of the Latin stressed vowels (i.e., vowels that bear the main accent in a word). Latin had ten distinct vowel sounds. The five letters, *a, e, i, o, u* represented the quality of the vowel. In addition, each vowel sound was pronounced as either *long* or *short*. This quantitative dimension was, to a large extent, lost in the evolution of Latin into its many Romance dialects, especially as a distinctive feature of vowels. In the Tuscan *volgare* the following two patterns of vocalic development stand out:

- The short Latin Ĕ and ŏ evolved generally into the diphthongs *ie* and *uo* respectively in open syllables (syllables that end with a vowel): TĔNE(T) ('s/he holds') > *tiene*; BŏNU(M) ('good') > *buono*.
- The short Latin ĭ and ŭ developed into *e* and *o* respectively: PĬRU(M) ('pear tree') > *pero*; GŭLA(M) ('throat') > *gola*.

Such facts can be used as templates for identifying dialectal differences. For example, none of the above changes occurred in Sicilian: *tene, bonu, piru, gula*. Another development that is useful in classifying the dialects is the phenomenon of **metaphony** – a characteristic that sets many southern dialects apart from standard Italian. This is defined as the process whereby the final vowel of a word affects the evolution of the vowel in the stressed syllable. Take, for instance, the outcomes of the following Latin words in Neapolitan (m = masculine; f = feminine; s = singular; pl = plural):

1. BONU(M) ('good') (m, s) > *buone* (the final *e* in Neapolitan is pronounced indistinctly, similar to the *e* in the *-er* ending in English *sender, lender,* etc.)
2. BONI (m, pl) > *buone*
3. BONA (f, s) > *bona*
4. BONÆ (f, pl) > *bone*
5. PORTU(M) ('port') (m, s) > *puorte*
6. PORTA(M) ('door') (f, s) > *porta*
7. RUSSU(M) ('red') (m, s) > *russe*
8. RUSSA(M) (f, s) > *rossa*

When compared with (3) and (4), examples (1) and (2) reveal that the final U and I of the Latin source word induced the diphthongization of the stressed vowel. The same applies to examples (5) and (6). Example (7) shows that the final U blocked the development of short ŭ > *o*, which is manifest in (8).

Incidentally, the same phonetic criteria that are used to classify the Eastern and Western Romance languages apply to Italian dialects as well: for example, in those dialects that lie to the north of the Gothic Line the processes of voicing and simplification emerge as characteristic. The Latin word FRATELLU(M) ('brother'), for instance, which became *fratello* in Tuscan, became *fradel* in Milanese. The latter form shows both phenomena, namely the voicing of intervocalic /t/ > /d/ and the simplification of /ll/ > /l/. However, it should be noted that none of the northern dialects at present employs the sigmatic plural, as do or did other Western Romance tongues.

Such historical criteria provide a comparative grid against which the various dialects can be put in order to identify their differences. In addition to phonetic, there are grammatical and lexical criteria that can be used to complete the grid. That is the task of the branch of linguistics known as **dialectology**. It is beyond the scope of the present discussion to enter into the details of how dialectologists construct the grid. Suffice it to say here that the comparative method used in this chapter illustratively allows them to establish, with some precision, the features that differentiate one dialect from another. The word *dialect*, incidentally, derives from Greek *dialektos* ('speech'), which itself is a compound of *dia-* ('between, over, across') and *legein* ('to speak'), a word that clearly refers to the phenomenon that language varies across geographical space.

To illustrate how dialectologists would draw up a dialectal map of Italy, known as a **dialect atlas**, one example will suffice. The Latin clusters /pl/, /fl/, and /kl/ have all undergone changes in the neo-Latin dialects in predictable ways. Here are some examples to show this (/ʃ/ = palatal sound similar to the *sh* in *shove*; /č/ = palatal sound similar to the *ch* in *birch*):

LATIN	TUSCAN	SICILIAN	LIGURIAN
CLAVE(M) *key*	*chiave* = [kyave]	[ʃavi]	[čav]
FLUME(N) *river*	*fiume* = [fyume]	[humi]	[ʃüme]
PLUMBU(M) *lead*	*piombo* = [pyombo]	[kyummu]	[čunĵu]

As this chart shows, in Tuscan the /l/ of the Latin clusters underwent vocalization: /kl/ > /ky/, /fl/ > /fy/, /pl/ > /py/; in Ligurian, the clusters underwent palatalization – that is, they evolved into palatal consonants, /ʃ/ or /č/; in Sicilian, the /kl/ also underwent palatalization to /ʃ/, but the /fl/ developed to /h/, and the /pl/ to /ky/. Now, a map of the Italian regions would show how these outcomes are distributed. By expanding the above chart to include the other dialects and the entire phonetic repertoire of Latin, the dialectologist would then be able to draw a fairly accurate picture of where the major dialectal areas are, according to specific traits.

Standard Italian

The many dialects spoken on the Italian peninsula have, until the advent of the 'TV age,' always presented a peculiar obstacle to the evolution of an accepted standard language that would reflect the cultural unity of the entire peninsula. As mentioned above, it was during the fourteenth century that the Tuscan neo-Latin dialect gained prominence, because of the central position of Tuscany in Italy, because of the aggressive commerce of its most important city, Florence, and because of the fame of Dante, Petrarca, and Boccaccio.

During the fifteenth and the sixteenth centuries, grammarians attempted to confer classical Latin features upon the pronunciation, grammar, and vocabulary of the Tuscan *volgare*. Eventually, this trend was widened to include the changes inevitable in a living tongue. In fact, in the dictionaries and publications of the **Accademia della Crusca,** founded in 1583, which came to be accepted by Italians as authoritative in linguistic matters, compromises between classical purism and living Tuscan usage were successfully effected. Compromise has always been the rule in Italy. In the standard language the Latin qualities of the Florentine dialect are preserved, but pronunciation and vocabulary have been allowed to change adaptively. As the great Spanish writer Miguel de Cervantes (1547–1616) wrote in his masterpiece *Don Quixote*, it is precisely in this way that languages are born: 'when the words are adopted by the multitude, and naturalized by custom' (vol. 2, book 6, chap. 10).

In effect, standard Italian is Florentine Tuscan that has been modified over the centuries and enriched from many linguistic sources. A salient Tuscan phonetic feature missing from the pronunciation of standard Italian, however, is the so-called *gorgia toscana*. This refers to the aspiration of certain consonants, especially /k/, between vowels. For example, the chart below shows the pronunciation of *la casa*, *l'oca*, and *poco* in Standard Italian and in Tuscan:

LATIN	TUSCAN	STANDARD ITALIAN
CASA(M)	la /hasa/	la /kasa/
OCA(M)	/oha/	/oka/
PAUCU(M)	/poho/	/poko/

It should be noted that this feature is not as prominent or as widespread within Tuscany as it once was, as younger speakers living in Tuscany today become increasingly influenced by the standard Italian modes of pronunciation to which they are constantly being exposed on television. Generally speaking, throughout Italy the characteristic features of dialectal pronunciation are steadily disappearing as a consequence of the influence that electronic media have had on speech habits.

Today, moreover, there is as much concern over the invasive nature of English into the Italian language as there was in the eighteenth century, when Alfieri and Parini protested against the invasion of French words and stylistic mannerisms into the language. Words like *sport, film, computer, software, hardware,* and *compact disc* have become as much a part of the Italian lexicon as any indigenous Latin word. But such words have not penetrated the essential character of the language. Interestingly, at present they have not undergone complete adaptation to Italian pronunciation and word structure, known as the process of **nativization** – for example, *film* should have become *filme.* The reason why such words have not been nativized is either because they have entered the language fairly recently, or because Italians today are consciously aware of their foreign nature and, for whatever reason, prefer to imitate their foreign pronunciation.

In fact, there have been perceived 'threats' to the language from foreign influence throughout the history of Italian. In addition to the widespread influence of French on Italian in the eighteenth century, as briefly noted above, Italian has endured quite a number of linguistic influences from the outside. Already in the Middle Ages, the prestige of Arabic scholarship led to the importation of words such as *albicocco* ('apricot tree'), *arsenale* ('arsenal'), *algebra, cifra* ('digit, number'), and *zero.* But such **borrowings**, as they are called, have hardly ever affected the structure of the original Tuscan *volgare.* The borrowed words, known as **loanwords**, were over time adapted to the sound patterns of the language by Italian speakers. This is why words like *cifra* and *zero* are no longer recognizable as foreign.

Characteristics

Lord Byron's reference to the satin quality of the Italian language with which we started this chapter was surely inspired by the fact that words in Italian end regularly in vowels, making it easy to rhyme them and thus create poetic expressions with relative ease.

Italian has, in fact, retained the final vowels that it inherited from Latin, changing, as we have seen, short ŭ to /o/ and æ to /e/:

1. VINŬ(M) ('wine') > *vino*
2. MUTA(T) ('s/he changes') > *muta*
3. PANE(M) ('bread') > *pane*
4. BONÆ ('good' f, pl) > *buone*

This salient characteristic of Italian words gives them a consonant–vowel flow – a kind of *ta-ta* rhythm that produces the impression of a steady beat to the words used in utterances. In the northern dialects, on the other hand, the final vowels are regularly dropped, so that most words end in a consonant (like French or English). For example, the equivalents of (1) and (3) above in Lombard are *vin* and *pan*.

Another phonetic feature that gives Italian its character is the presence of double consonants: *tutto, bello, anno, carro, osso,* and so on. This trait is found in the central and southern dialects, too, but not in those north of the Gothic Line: for example, in Bolognese the counterpart of *carro* ('cart') is *car*.

Many more traits of pronunciation, grammar, and vocabulary differentiate Italian from the other Romance languages and from other dialects within Italy. It is not possible to go into any appreciable detail here. Suffice it to say that Italian, like any language or dialect, has its own recognizable physiognomy, and this can be described as concretely as can a face, an arm, or some other feature of corporeal physiognomy. The goal of subsequent chapters, thus, is to describe some of the physical features of Italian.

Some of these will, of course, be seen to resemble those of other languages. If mutual intelligibility is the basic criterion, current estimates indicate that about 6,000 languages are spoken in the world today. Linguists classify languages using two main methods: the **typological** method classifies languages according to their structural features, while the **genetic** method classifies languages into families on the basis of their historical genealogy.

Typologically, Italian is both an *inflectional* and *word-order* language. Like its progenitor, Latin, Italian shows various grammatical relations by **inflection**, that is, by variations or changes that its words undergo to indicate their relations with other words and changes in meaning. Inflection includes the conjugation of verbs, the declension of nouns and adjectives, and the modification of adjectival forms (e.g., *big, bigger, biggest*). Although Latin was marked by elaborate systems of inflections, these were simplified considerably over time in Italian. In many cases, the word order in a sentence has taken over the functions of some of Latin's inflections. In Latin, the sentence *The boy* (PUER) *loves* (AMAT) *the girl* (PUELLAM) could have been rendered in any one of six ways because the ending of each word informs the speaker or listener what relation each has to the others: PUER is in the nominative case and is thus interpreted as the subject of the sentence; PUELLAM is in the accusative form (nominative = PUELLA) and thus is interpreted as the object of the sentence, no matter where it occurs:

1. PUER   AMAT   PUELLAM
2. PUER   PUELLAM   AMAT
3. AMAT   PUER   PUELLAM
4. AMAT   PUELLAM   PUER
5. PUELLAM   AMAT   PUER
6. PUELLAM   PUER   AMAT

In Italian, this is not the case. *Il ragazzo ama la ragazza* and *La ragazza ama il ragazzo* mean different things. Nevertheless, some of the flexibility of Latin syntax is found in Italian to this day: for example, although the sequences *Il ragazzo, la ragazza ama* and *Ama la ragazza, il ragazzo* sound a bit awkward, they are still possible versions of the same sentence. Overall, however, Italian depends much more on word order for establishing meaning than did its parent language.

Genetically, as we have seen, Italian belongs to the Romance family of languages, all descended from Latin, which was, itself, an Indo-European language. The Indo-European languages constitute the most widely spoken languages in Europe. The family contains a number of subfamilies, including the Germanic languages, in addition to the Romance languages. The Indo-Iranian language group is another major branch of the Indo-European family. It has two subbranches, Iranian and Indo-Aryan, which are spoken from southwest Asia through much of the Indian subcontinent.

Italian is continually undergoing changes, although its speakers are usually unaware of the changes as they occur. Historical change can affect all components of language. We saw how sound change has occurred in the development of Italian and the other Romance languages. Change can also affect grammar and the meaning of words. A classic example is the meaning of the word *persona* ('person'). In Etruscan, and initially in Latin, it meant a mask worn by actors on a stage for portraying character. In time it came to have the meaning of the *character* of the actor wearing the mask. This designation is still found in the term *dramatis personae,* the cast of characters of a play. Subsequently, it came to have the meaning of individual character. Here are a few other examples of how the meanings of certain words have changed:

	ORIGINAL MEANING	ITALIAN FORM	NEW MEANING
DOMU(S)	*house*	duomo	*cathedral*
CASA(M)	*shack*	casa	*house*
CABALLU(S)	*type of horse*	cavallo	*horse (in general)*

Follow-Up Activities

1. Do you agree with Lord Byron's description of Italian as having a 'satin' quality? Elaborate on your answer.

2. Define the following terms and notions in your own words:

Romance language
dialect
assimilation
vocalization
palatalization
neo-Latin dialect
vulgar Latin
Appendix Probi
Gothic Line
voicing
simplification
sigmatic plural
volgare
volgare illustre
lingua letteraria
questione della lingua
dolce stil nuovo
Arcadia
verismo
neorealism
metaphony
dialectology
dialect atlas
Accademia della Crusca
gorgia toscana
nativization
borrowing

loanword
typological classification
genetic classification
inflection

3. To what language family does Italian belong?

4. From which language does it derive?

5. Given the following Latin words, provide their probable modern Italian versions, explaining to the best of your ability, the changes that have occurred.

   Example: actu(m) ('act') > *atto* (assimilation of /kt/ > /tt/)

   CRŬCE(M) ('cross')
   PRATU(M) ('field')
   NASU(M) ('nose')
   STRATA(M) ('road')
   NĬVE(M) ('snow')
   NŬCE(M) ('walnut')
   CAUDA(M) ('tail')
   MATRE(M) ('mother')
   PATRE(M) ('father')
   PĔDE(M) ('foot')
   HŎMO ('man')
   FLŌRE(M) ('flower')
   PATELLA(M) ('pan')
   FĬCATU(M) ('liver')
   CLAVE(M) ('key')
   PLĒNU(M) ('full')

6. What kinds of evidence are used to reconstruct vulgar Latin?

7. What are some of the linguistic features used for classifying a Romance language as Western or Eastern?

8. Summarize the characteristics that make the *Indovinello veronese* an early text written in *volgare*.

9. Give reasons why the Tuscan *volgare* became the basis for standard Italian.

10. How are the Italian dialects classified?

11. Give examples of metaphony in any dialect you may know. If you do not know one, then compile a brief list of metaphonically derived words by interviewing a native speaker of a southern Italian dialect, asking her or him to give you the corresponding words for *buono, buoni, buona, buone, porto, porta, rosso,* and *rossa*.

12. Describe briefly in your own words how standard Italian came into being.

13. Look up the following words and indicate if they are derived directly from Latin or from some foreign source.

    Example: ammiraglio ('admiral')
                 from Arabic *amìrâlì* ('high commander')

    amico
    verità
    jazz
    secchio
    nome
    footing
    programma

14. What are some features that differentiate Italian from other Romance languages?

2
Linguistics

....

Science is organized knowledge.

Herbert Spencer (1820–1903)

Recall from the previous chapter that the technique of comparative
analysis allowed us to determine two things at once: that the languages
being compared (Italian, French, Spanish) were related genetically (as
descendants of Latin), and that precise correspondences among the
three in a particular area of pronunciation could be established. In microcosm, that simple procedure reflects how **linguistics** as a science
originated in the nineteenth century. Known, logically, as the **comparative** method, it allowed scholars to determine phonetic relationships
among languages and to discover how different languages may have influenced one another in their development.

The comparative study of languages actually traces its starting point
to 1786, when the English scholar Sir William Jones suggested the possible affinity of Sanskrit and Persian with Greek and Latin. For the first
time, someone had brought to scientific light the possibility of genetic
relations among languages. With Jones's revelation, the school of *comparative linguistics* began, a school that did much to establish the existence of the Indo-European family of languages and to create a basis
for a scientific study of language.

In the opening chapter, we also looked at the features of standard
Italian that set it apart, historically, from the Italian dialects and from
other Romance languages. This allowed us to look at the Italian language 'objectively' – without any bias as to any aesthetic qualities it is
purported to have or not to have. Interestingly, Dante had himself described the complex Italian linguistic situation in his famous *De vulgari*

eloquentiae ('Of Vulgar Tongues'), starting a debate on what constituted the proper linguistic basis for standard Italian. The *questione della lingua*, as it came to be called, was never really resolved until a late-nineteenth-century scholar, named G.I. Ascoli, began to describe and classify the Italian dialects geographically on the basis of the historical correspondences that existed among the dialects.

Like any scientific methodology, linguistic analysis is based on observation, data collection, description, investigation, and the theoretical explanation of phenomena. It does not make blanket statements about what is 'good grammar,' as do the many kinds of grammatical texts used in schools. It does not espouse a *normative*, or *prescriptive*, approach to language, but a *descriptive* one. Linguists study not only standard usage, but also the geographical and social variation that ensues from the use of language in everyday life. They are concerned both with describing the structure of language, and with how language is used in society, how it is learned, and how it changes over time.

The study of the latter – how language changes – is called **diachronic analysis**. The description of language as it is spoken at a particular point in time, normally the present, is called **synchronic analysis**. The essence of synchronic analysis lies in determining how best to describe the sounds, word-building units, sentence patterns, and discourse structures that characterize a language. That will be, in effect, the objective of subsequent chapters. The purpose of this one is simply to discuss briefly, by illustration, what linguistics is basically about. We will start with a brief historical overview of linguistic science. Then, we will look at the various aspects of language that linguists focus on – phonology, morphology, syntax, semantics, discourse, and variation.

Historical Overview

One of the first attempts in history to study a language scientifically can be traced as far back as the fifth century BC, when the Indian scholar Panini compiled a grammar of the Sanskrit language of India. His sophisticated analysis, which he wrote as a linguistic guide to the interpretation of Hindu religious literature written in Sanskrit, showed how words are formed systematically from smaller units. The Greek grammarian Dionysius Thrax, who lived between 170 and 90 BC, wrote what became one of the first influential models for writing grammars in Europe, the *Art of Grammar*. Many later Greek, Latin, and other European grammars were based on his model.

With the spread of Christianity and the translation of the Scriptures into the languages of the new Christians, written literatures began to develop among previously nonliterate peoples. This led to an interest in grammatical analysis and description as a formal approach to the general study of languages. The Arabs are believed to have begun the serious grammatical study of their language before medieval times. In the tenth century the Jews completed a Hebrew lexicon and grammar, based on solid principles of analysis and description. By the late Middle Ages, European scholars generally knew, in addition to their own languages and Latin, the tongues of their nearest neighbours.

The access to several languages set scholars to thinking about how languages might be compared. The revival of classical learning in the Renaissance, however, led many grammarians to go against the previous grain as they attempted to fit the grammatical facts of different languages into the theoretical framework of Greek and Latin grammar. It was in the sixteenth and seventeenth centuries that scholars found this to be a misguided course of grammatical inquiry, taking it upon themselves to make the first in-depth surveys of all the then-known languages in an attempt to determine which grammatical facts were universal and which were specific to different languages. In the eighteenth century the comparisons were becoming increasingly precise, culminating in the assumption by the German philosopher Gottfried Wilhelm Leibniz that most languages of Europe, Asia, and Egypt came from the same original language – a language referred to as *Indo-European*.

In the nineteenth century, scholars carried out systematic analyses of the parts of speech, mostly built on the earlier analyses of Sanskrit by Panini. This established a precise method for comparing and relating the forms of speech in numerous languages. As mentioned, Sir William Jones observed that Sanskrit bore similarities to Greek and Latin, and proposed that the three languages might have developed from a common source. Inspired by Jones, language scholars in the nineteenth century started in earnest to compare languages. Jacob Grimm, the German philologist (one who studies the language of old texts), and Rasmus Christian Rask, a Danish philologist, noted that when the sounds of one language corresponded in a regular way to similar sounds in related words in another language, the correspondences were consistent. For example, they found that the initial sounds of Latin PATER ('father') and PED- ('foot') corresponded regularly to English *father* and *foot*.

By the late nineteenth century, much research had been conducted on sound correspondences. A group of European language scholars known as the *neogrammarians* then put forward the view that not only were sound correspondences between related languages regular, but any exceptions to these could develop only from borrowings from another language (or from additional sound changes). For example, Latin /d/ should correspond to English /t/ as in DENTALIS = *tooth*. The English word *dental*, however, has a /d/ sound. The conclusion drawn by the neogrammarians was that English borrowed *dental* from Latin, whereas *tooth* (which has the expected /t/) was a native English word.

It was the Swiss linguist Ferdinand de Saussure who founded modern linguistic methodology in the same century when he proposed that a distinction be made between diachronic facts and synchronic aspects of language study. Saussure advanced the view of language as a system of structures serving as links between thought and vocal expression. His approach came to be known as **structuralism**. The central notion of structuralism is a distinction between *langue* (French for 'language'), denoting the system underlying a particular language, namely, what members of a speech community speak and hear that will pass as acceptable grammar to other speakers and hearers of that language – and *parole* (French for 'word'), which denotes the actual speech forms that represent instances of *langue*. The structuralist approach conceives of *langue* as a system of elements at various levels – sound, word, sentence, meaning – that are interconnected in a systematic fashion. It is this interconnection that produces meaning, not the elements in isolation. A structuralist **grammar** therefore describes the relationships that underlie all instances of speech in a particular language.

Saussure used the analogy of a chess game to illustrate analogically the difference between *langue* and *parole*. Chess can be played only by two people who know the rules of the game. This constitutes knowledge of chess, *langue*, which includes knowing how to move the pieces on the board, which moves are strategic and which are not, no matter what size the board, what substance the pieces are made of, and so on. Now, the actual use of this knowledge to play a specific game of chess is *parole*. This involves knowing how to apply the rules to respond to certain moves of the opponent.

In America, the structuralist approach was adopted in the early twentieth century by the anthropologist Franz Boas and his student Edward Sapir, who worked primarily with Native American languages, and a little later by Leonard Bloomfield, whose book titled *Language* (1933) established the basic notions and procedures for carrying out a structuralist analysis of any language. Boas was especially influential in establishing linguistics as a science. He saw the goal of linguistics as the description of how socially based speech is organized grammatically. A structural grammar, Boas claimed, should describe the relationships of speech elements in words and sentences as they are used in actual society. Given impetus by the fresh perspective of Boas, structuralism became dominant in the United States during the first half of the twentieth century. The essence of structuralist linguistic methodology was the gathering of data from native speakers and its classification and analysis in terms of separate levels (phonology, morphology, syntax, semantics). At about the same time, the influential Danish linguist Otto Jespersen, like Boas, stressed that grammar should be studied by examining living speech rather than by analysing written documents. Jespersen also wanted to ascertain what principles were common to the grammars of all languages.

The first major break from structuralism came in 1957, when the American linguist Noam Chomsky published a book titled simply *Syntactic Structures*, in which he analysed the syntax of English from a different perspective than the structuralist one, known as **generative**. Generative grammar is an approach that focuses on syntax as the central feature of linguistic competence. The goal of linguistics, according to Chomsky, should be the analysis of the innate capacity of the human infant to produce and understand well-formed sentences in the language to which he or she is exposed at birth. Chomsky's view was not without precedent, however. It was in line with the tradition established by various eighteenth- and early-nineteenth-century scholars who claimed that grammatical forms were reflexes of innate logic forms. For instance, the British philosopher John Stuart Mill, writing in 1867, believed that the rules of grammar corresponded to universal logical forms. Chomsky simply went one step further, suggesting that such forms were the products of a **universal grammar** present in the brain at birth and of a capacity for acquiring the rules of grammar of particular languages. Since the late 1960s various schools of linguistics have come forward to challenge the Chomskyan perspective. These cannot be discussed here due to lack of space. Suffice it to say that current linguistic theory and methodology have become more eclectic and less partisan to one school of thought than they ever were at any time in the twentieth century.

Currently, approaches in linguistics are divided into theoretical or applied. *Theoretical* linguistics is concerned with building language models or theories to describe languages or to explain the nature of their structures. *Applied* linguists, on the other hand, apply the findings of linguistics to language teaching, dictionary preparation, speech therapy, computerized machine translation, and automatic speech recognition. A number of linguistic fields are concerned with the relations between language and the subject matter of related academic disciplines, such as *sociolinguistics* (sociology and language), *psycholinguistics* (psychology and language), and *neurolinguistics* (neuropsychology and language).

But in all approaches, versions, fields, and subfields, certain notions and techniques have stood the test of time and now constitute a standard repository of procedures for the scientific study of languages. These include describing a language's sounds (*phonetics* and *phonology*), words (*morphology*), relations among words in a sentence (*syntax*), meaning patterns (*semantics*), and variation according to the contexts in which a language is used or applied (*pragmatics*, or *discourse analysis*).

Phonology

A language is a system made up of subsystems (of sound, word formation, etc.) connected to each other in patterned ways. The systematicity of language structure can easily be seen by purposely introducing errors into some specific subsystem of a language. This allows one to focus on 'what has gone wrong,' and, thus, to flesh out what structural principle has been breached (and hence to consciously grasp that principle).

Take, for example, the following sequence of words:

Il pfambino simpatico mangia la caramella

Any native speaker of Italian, or indeed anyone who has studied the language even at an elementary level, can instantly point to the word *pfambino* as decidedly 'un-Italian.' The other words, and the sentence itself, are otherwise 'well-formed.' Now, the question becomes: Why is the word *pfambino* un-Italian? To a linguist, the answer is to be found at the level of the sound system of Italian, known as the level of **phonology**. What specific aspect of phonological structure, the linguist would then ask, does the word *pfambino* violate? Taken separately, each sound is a legitimate one in Italian:

- The initial *p* is found in words such as *pane, palla, pieno,* etc.
- The *f* is found in *forte, fisica, fieno,* etc.
- The *a* is found in *anno, amica, arte,* etc.
- The *m* is found in *mamma, mica, muro,* etc.
- The *b* is found in *balla, bere, bene,* etc.
- The *i* is found in *inno, isola, ieri,* etc.
- The *n* is found in *nonno, nove, notte,* etc.
- The *o* is found in *osso, ora, otto,* etc.

The problem, clearly, is not one of a foreign sound having been inserted into the formation of this word. Foreign sounds often do make their way into Italian, but not in the formation of words. They come as part and parcel of a borrowed word. Rather, the problem with the legitimacy of this word appears to be in a specific combination of sounds. In fact, the sequence *pf* violates consonant cluster structure at the beginning of words. So, the appropriate diagnosis of the error points to a violation of a specific kind of structure. Note that this is not a violation of *universal cluster-formation structure*. Indeed, this very cluster is found in German in initial position: *Pferd* = 'horse.'

This diagnostic analysis has opened up a small window showing how phonological subsystems are structured. The task of the linguist, however, is not only to account for how sounds are combined in clusters, but also how they are used to convey meaning. Only a fraction of the sounds humans are physiologically capable of articulating are found in any particular language. For example, Italian lacks the sounds represented by *th* in *thing* and *that*, which are articulated by sticking the tongue out (between the teeth); it also lacks the aspirated *h* sound in words like *horse* and *house*. Note that the *h* used to write words like *ho, hai, ha, hanno* does not represent any sound – it is like the 'silent *h*' of English *hour* and *honour*.

Some of the objectives of a linguistic analysis of Italian phonology would thus include:

- Describing and classifying its vowels, consonants, and other kinds of sounds.
- Describing the structure of its syllables.

• Relating sounds to their orthographic representation.

Morphology

Obviously, the correct word that should have been used in the sentence above is *bambino*. Now, let us return to that same sequence and introduce another kind of error:

Il bambino simpatica mangia la caramella

Once again, to a native speaker of Italian, it is a simple matter to spot the error. The word *simpatica* should end in -*o* rather than in -*a*. Note that this is not a phonological error, like the one above, because, taken in isolation, the form *simpatica* is a legitimate, well-formed word that occurs in phrases such as the following:

• *la bambina simpatica*
• *la donna simpatica*
• *la madre simpatica*
• *la nonna simpatica*

So, what aspect of Italian language structure does the word *simpatica* violate in this specific sentence? The answer is to be found by considering the **morphological** subsystem of Italian, the level at which words are given their particular shape and are made to agree in form with one another. In the above case, the problem is one of 'morphological agreement': the adjective form *simpatica* is used with nouns marked as feminine. Changing the ending to -*o* produces the appropriate form to be used with a masculine noun like *bambino* – *Il bambino simpatico mangia la caramella*.

The study of morphological subsystems includes determining what constitutes a word and what units (smaller than words) convey meaning. The English word *birds*, for instance, can be split morphologically into the word *bird* and the ending -*s*. The former bears dictionary meaning; the latter has a purely grammatical meaning (plural). Words are *minimal free forms*, but a word may contain one or more *bound* forms. The endings -*o* and -*a* in Italian are examples of such forms.

The particular characteristics of a language's morphological subsystem often provide the criteria for relating languages typologically. Languages can be classified according to the number of bound forms per word. In **analytic** languages, such as Chinese, words tend to be free forms, while in **synthetic** languages, such as Italian, one word may contain several bound forms. In the case of some Native American languages, a single word may have so many component units that it is the equivalent of an English sentence.

A study of the morphological system of Italian would include, minimally, the following tasks:

- An analysis of the pluralization of nouns (*libro → libri, penna → penne*, etc.).
- A description of the agreement patterns between nouns and adjectives (*il bambino simpatico, la bambina simpatica*).
- An account of the inflection patterns related to articles, demonstratives, etc. (*il ragazzo, uno zio,* etc.).
- An analysis of verbal tense and mood forms (*mangio, mangiavo,* etc.).
- A description of affixation (*logico → illogico, alto → altamente,* etc.).

Syntax

Now, consider the following sequence of the same words:

Bambino simpatico il mangia caramella la

Clearly, there are no errors in this sequence that transgress either phonological or morphological structure – indeed, all the words in the sequence above are well formed phonologically and morphologically. A native speaker will instantly point out that the two articles are 'out of place' because in Italian articles must precede nouns and adjectives, not follow them. Any other arrangement constitutes an error in **syntax**, the level at which words and units are organized into phrases and sentences. Note that the 'post-positioning' of the article is an acceptable syntactic pattern in other languages, such as Rumanian: *casa* ('the house') → *casele* ('the houses').

In syntactic analysis the primary task is to describe the structure of phrases and sentences in terms of how they are organized in sentences. For example, our illustrative sentence would show two basic or primary constituents, *il bambino simpatico* and *mangia la caramella*. This basic organizational feature can be shown with a 'tree diagram' as follows:

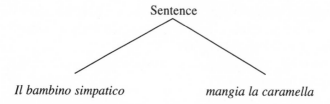

The constituent to the left (as one looks at the diagram from above the page) is known as the *subject* of the sentence; the constituent to the right is known as the *predicate*. Now, each primary constituent may be broken down into a series of secondary and tertiary constituents. The phrase *il bambino simpatico* is a noun phrase made up of an article, a noun, and an adjective. The predicate, on the other hand, is made up of two secondary constituents, a verb and a following noun phrase, known as an *object*. The latter can be decomposed further into an article and a noun:

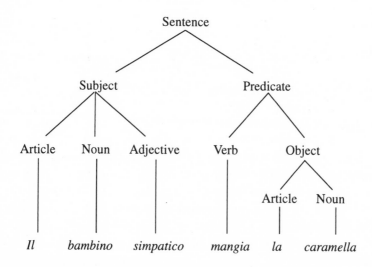

The above diagram shows clearly how the parts relate to each other in a 'hierarchical' fashion. Syntactic structure is not linear, the result of simply putting one word next to another, but the result of organizing words in such a way that they relate to each other hierarchically.

The analysis of Italian syntax would include a study of:

- Basic phrase structure.
- The ordering of the words within phrases.
- Agreement between entities (e.g., agreement of number and gender between subject and verb).
- Case structure (position and function of a word within a sentence).
- Sentence types (e.g., negatives, interrogatives, etc.).

Semantics

So far we have been concerned with infringements of some aspect of the 'well-formedness' of consonant clusters, words, and sentence structure. Now, consider the following version of our sentence, which is well formed at all levels, but which still presents an anomaly:

Il bambino beve la caramella

Because the sentence is well formed, we are inclined to find a meaning for it. But real-world experience tells us that *caramelle* are normally eaten, not drunk. In essence, this sentence has no real-life meaning, although a scenario in which a candy may be ingested with a buccal action that resembles drinking can always be imagined. The gist of the above illustration is that there exists a level of meaning, known as the **semantic** level, in which words and phrases relate to each other in terms of what they actually stand for. The semantic system is the bridge between language as a representational system and the world of feelings, experiences, ideas, and so on.

The study of semantic subsystems has three basic concerns: the relations of words to the objects denoted by them, the relations of words to their interpreters, and the formal relations of words and phrases to one another. An interesting aspect of semantic subsystems is that they do not cover the same 'cognitive terrain,' so to speak. Even in naming a simple object, it would appear that each language does so in ways that are relative to its structure, its lexical resources, and most important, historical events related to the concept in question. Consider, for instance, the way in which an object that marks the passage of time is named in English and Italian. In the former language it is called *watch* if it is a carryable object and worn on the human body, usually on the wrist, but it is called *clock* if it is not a carryable object, and usually put in a place (e.g., a table) or hung from somewhere. In Italian no such semantic distinction applies. The word *orologio* means both *watch* and *clock*. This does not mean that Italian does not have the linguistic resources for making the distinction, if needed. Indeed, the phrase *da* + *place* allows speakers to provide exactly this kind of information:

- *orologio da polso* = wrist watch
- *orologio da tavolo* = table clock
- *orologio da muro* = wall clock

The difference between English and Italian in this specific semantic domain is that the former predisposes speakers to anticipate a distinction related to the carryability of the timepiece, while the latter does not. In effect, the semantic subsystems of the two languages have encoded a specific kind of meaning in different ways. Once established and acquired in social context, these meanings then become perceptual templates for the interpretation of experiences. In a phrase, language influences some aspects of thought.

The analysis of Italian semantics would include a study of:

- Basic and extended word meanings.
- Meaning relations (synonymy, antonymy, etc.).
- The relation of meanings among words in a sentence.

Discourse

Let us assume, for the sake of argument, that the sentence *Il bambino mangia la caramella* is uttered in response to different kinds of questions:

1.
Question: Che fa quel bambino?
Answer: (Il bambino) mangia la caramella.

2.
Question: È vero che quel bambino mangia la caramella?
Answer: (Sì, è vero.) Il bambino mangia la caramella.

3.
Question: Chi mangia la caramella, il bambino o la bambina?
Answer: Il bambino (mangia la caramella).

As an answer in (1), our sentence, *Il bambino mangia la caramella*, is intended to provide a simple, straightforward information exchange. The questioner asks what the boy is doing, and the respondent refers directly to the boy's actions. As an answer in (2), it has a different function: it is intended as a confirmation of what the questioner asks, not as a conveyance of new information. As an answer in (3), our sentence identifies which of the two alternatives to which the questioner refers is the appropriate one.

Our sentence can assume many more functions and meanings – it all depends on the nature of the **discourse** situation, that is, on the social context in which it is uttered. The branch of linguistics that studies discourse phenomena, and their effect on the decipherment of meaning, is called **pragmatics**, or *discourse analysis*. Pragmatic research has shown how language is a malleable instrument, constantly adaptable to changing needs and social situations, and especially to the intent of the speaker.

The situational context provides the critical semantic cues and formats for interpreting sentences. In the early 1970s, the linguist Dell Hymes challenged the Chomskyan idea of **linguistic competence** as a form of innate knowledge that was considered at the time to be impervious to influences from real-world communication and social interaction. He proposed that knowledge of language entailed the ability to use it appropriately in specific social and interactive settings. He called this kind of knowledge **communicative competence**, claiming that it even had an effect in shaping and changing linguistic competence. Studies on the nature of communication and discourse proliferated shortly thereafter.

The common factor in all pragmatic studies is the utilization of speech act theories as the organizing frameworks for understanding language use. The concept of **speech act** is an interesting one. It can be defined as knowledge of how to match words to a situation so that some meaning exchange can be literally 'acted out' in a socially appropriate fashion. A simple protocol like saying hello, for instance, requires a detailed knowledge of the appropriate words, phrases, structures, and nonverbal cues that come together cohesively in a script-like fashion to enable a speaker to make successful social contact with another speaker. It requires, in other words, both *procedural* and *linguistic* knowledge. An infringement of any of the procedural details of this script might lead to a breakdown in communication. In speech act theory, language form (grammar and vocabulary) is seen as the servant of communication (procedural knowledge).

The study of Italian discourse would include such topics as:

- speech acts
- conversational devices
- the relation of conversation to gesture
- how information is communicated in specific situations
- the relation between narrative and discourse

Variation

As a final consideration, it is significant to note that the way in which our sentence *(Il bambino mangia la caramella)* would be delivered phonetically by actual speakers would vary regionally. Speakers from north of the Gothic Line would tend to pronounce the /ll/ in *caramella* with a single /l/; speakers in Naples would probably render the final vowels as slightly indistinct *schwa* sounds, (like the *e* in English *waiter*, *lover*, etc.). Although, as mentioned in the opening chapter, such differences are being levelled today, vestiges of dialectal pronunciation habits can still be heard, even if more and more sporadically.

Within a speech community there is considerable **variation** in a language. The way people speak will vary not only according to where they live, but also according to their age, occupation, socioeconomic status, gender, and so forth. As we saw in the previous chapter, variation according to region is called *dialectal*. In fact, linguists speak of both *regional* or *geographical dialects* and of *social dialects*. The latter term was coined to refer to variation along a social axis: for example, the way teenagers talk among themselves is different from how university professors talk to each other.

An interesting aspect of variation is the phenomenon of *language styles*, or **registers**. These are forms of speech that are made to fit the formality of the situation, the medium used (speech or writing), and the topic under discussion. Take, for example, saying good-bye to another person in Italian. This will vary as follows:

Highly formal:	ArrivederLa
Mid-formal:	Arrivederci
Informal:	Ciao

The choice of one or the other is a matter of politeness. In Italy, these registers are maintained in daily conversations, not to signal class but to convey level of formality. In some societies, such as in Java, registers are tied to social groups. At the top of the social hierarchy are the aristocrats, in the middle the townsfolk, and at the bottom the farmers. Each of these has a distinct style of speech associated with it. The top register is used by aristocrats who do not know one another very well, but also by a member of the townsfolk if he or she happens to be addressing a highly placed government official. The middle register is used by townsfolk who are not friends, and by peasants when addressing their social superiors. The low register is used by peasants, or by an aristocrat or townsperson talking to a peasant, and among friends on any level; it is also the form of language used to speak to children.

Included among the phenomena that can be studied with regard to variation in the Italian language are the following:

- geographically based variation
- variation in social groups
- variation in the language spoken outside of Italy

Follow-Up Activities

1. Define the following terms and notions in your own words:

   linguistics
   comparative method
   diachronic analysis
   synchronic analysis
   structuralism
   langue
   parole
   grammar
   generative syntax
   universal grammar
   phonology
   morphology
   analytic language
   synthetic language
   syntax

semantics
discourse
pragmatics
linguistic competence
communicative competence
speech act
variation
register

2. After having read this chapter, how would you characterize linguistic methodology?

3. State the importance of the following in the history of linguistics:

Panini
Dionysius Thrax
grammatical study in the Middle Ages
Jacob Grimm
Rasmus Christian Rask
neogrammarians
Ferdinand de Saussure
Franz Boas
Edward Sapir
Leonard Bloomfield
Otto Jespersen
Noam Chomsky
Dell Hymes
G.I. Ascoli
Dante

4. In your own words, explain the difference between *langue* and *parole*.

5. What is the difference between theoretical and applied linguistics?

6. Determine in your own way what features of Italian phonology the following words violate:

Example: thicuro
The sound represented by *th* does not exist in Italian.

ktaccaio
thorto
cartu
spturo
coourso

7. What aspects of Italian sounds would a phonological analysis aim to study?

8. Determine in your own way what features of Italian morphology the following examples violate:

Example: le madre
Either the article form should be *la* in front of the singular form *madre*, or the noun should be pluralized to *madri*.

lo ragazzo
lo studenti
i libre
le ragazze francese
inlogico
precisomente

9. What would a morphological analysis of Italian include?

10. Determine in your own way what features of Italian syntax the following examples violate:

Example: Lui è ragazzo bravo un
The article is out of place: *Lui è un ragazzo bravo.*

bambino questo beve il latte.
Alessandro scuola a va ogni giorno.
mangia la ragazza la caramella.
andare il bambino deve a scuola.
piace gli la pizza.

11. What would a syntactic analysis of Italian include?

12. Point out any semantic differences between the following pairs of terms, one Italian and the other English:

   Example: libreria – library
   libreria is a book store; *biblioteca* is the word that corresponds to *library*

   azzurro – blue
   educazione – education
   sensibile – sensible
   bravo – good
   buono – good
   simpatico – nice
   fantasia – fantasy

13. What would a semantic analysis of Italian include?

14. Identify what is wrong in each of the following statements, in pragmatic terms.

   Example: Ciao, signore, come stai?
   The use of the informal items *ciao* and *stai* when talking to someone with whom one is not on a first-name basis.

   Signora, dove abiti?
   Marco, stia zitto!
   Signor Dini, sta' zitto!
   Mamma, Le dico che sono stanco!

15. What would a discourse analysis of Italian include?

16. Explain the difference between procedural and linguistic knowledge.

17. Explain the following in pragmatic, dialectal, or stylistic terms.

Example: Ciao – Buongiorno
Ciao is an informal way to greet someone in the morning; *buon-giorno* is a formal way to carry out the same social function.

Il bambino mangia la caramella – U picciriddu mangia a caramella.
Cerchi qualcosa? – Desidera?
Mi piace il cocomero – Mi piace l'anguria.
Come ti chiami? – Come si chiama?

18. What would a variation analysis of Italian include?

3

The Sounds of Italian

Language most shews a man: Speak, that I may see thee.

Ben Jonson (1573–1637)

The scientific study of a language starts typically with a careful examination of its sound system, the key to unlocking how its other systems and subsystems are interconnected. In order to do so, an unambiguous and consistent method of representing speech sounds is required. Alphabet characters are generally unreliable, because they do not always provide a guide to the actual pronunciation.

As an example, consider the ways in which the 'f' sound is represented alphabetically in English:

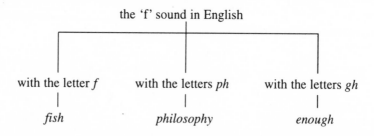

Although Italian orthography is much more consistent in representing sounds, it is not without its anomalies: for example, the *h* in *ho* and *hai* is not pronounced, and the letter *c* represents different sounds in *cena* and *cane*. Clearly, then, written forms are not only unreliable guides to actual pronunciation but may even obscure what the pronunciation really is. This is why, in order to study the sounds of a language, linguists abandon the use of conventional spelling symbols and adopt specially devised systems of notation in which one symbol represents one sound. The symbol [f] between square brackets, for instance, is the one used by linguists to indicate the 'f' sound represented vicariously by the letters *f, ph,* and *gh* in the above words.

The study of sound systems falls into five areas: (1) the actual physical description of the sounds, known as *phonetics*; (2) the analysis of how these constitute a subsystem in a language, known as *phonology*; (3) the description of syllable structure; (4) the study of intonation features, stress patterns, and so on, known as *prosodic analysis*; and (5) the comparison of the sounds with spelling symbols, known as *orthographic analysis*. We will deal with (2) in the next chapter. In this one, we will focus on the other four areas.

Phonetic Description

Phonetics is the branch of linguistics concerned with investigating and describing the production, physical nature, and perception of speech sounds. Phonetics has two main sub-branches: **articulatory** and **acoustic phonetics**. The former is concerned with cataloguing the physical activities of the vocal organs as they are used by speakers to modify the airstream in the mouth, nose, and throat in order to produce sounds. Phonetic symbols and their articulatory definitions are essentially abbreviated descriptions of these activities. The symbols most commonly used are those established by the International Phonetic Association (IPA) in 1886. These are written in brackets in order to differentiate them from alphabet characters. Acoustic phonetics is concerned with studying the pattern of speech waves associated with sounds. Here, we will deal only with the articulatory aspects of Italian sounds.

The use of a uniform set of symbols to represent speech sounds is the essence of phonetic description. Each symbol stands for only one sound. The [f] symbol mentioned above, for instance, stands for the sound formed (1) by the lower lip touching the upper teeth; (2) as the airstream emanating from the lungs is expelled in a constricted fashion through the mouth; and (3) with no vibration of the vocal cords (in the larynx). To render the description more efficient, it is useful to refer to these articulatory activities in a terminologically consistent way. This can done by designating feature (1) as *voiceless*, (2) as *labiodental*, and (3) as *fricative*. Thus, the sound [f], known more technically as a *phone*, is defined as a *voiceless labiodental fricative*. No matter how it is represented in spelling practices, the [f] symbol will always inform the analyst that the sound involved is a voiceless labiodental fricative.

This definition of [f] constitutes, in effect, a precise set of articulatory instructions that, like the instructions used in computer programs, reveal exactly how a sound is produced. The goal of phonetic description is to come up with a set of instructions for producing all possible sounds with the vocal apparatus. To do this, an understanding of the basic anatomical and physiological components of this apparatus is essential (see Figure 3.1 on p. 47).

The organs of articulation are either movable or stationary. Movable organs are the lips, jaws, tongue, and vocal cords. These modify the flow of air from the lungs. Stationary organs include the teeth, the alveolar arch behind them, the hard palate, and the softer velum behind it. Sounds made by touching two movable organs – for example, the [p] of *pane*, which requires both lips – or those made by means of a movable and a stationary part of the vocal apparatus are named in terms of the organs that make the juncture, which is called the **point of articulation**. Reference to the tongue, when it is an articulator, is not generally made – for example, the English [t] sound, which is produced with the tongue touching the alveolar arch, is called simply *alveolar*.

The way in which the airstream is modified by the movable organs is called the **manner of articulation**. This may entail: (1) stopping the air completely, as in the [p] of *pane*; (2) leaving the nasal passage open during the stoppage, as in the [n] of *naso*; (3) making contact with the tongue but leaving space on either side of it, as in the [l] of *latte*; (4) making a light contact, as in the [r] in *raro*; (5) leaving just enough space to allow the airstream to cause friction as it passes through, as in the [f] in *fatto*; or (6) permitting the airstream to pass over the centre of the tongue without oral friction, as in the [a] in *cane*.

The Vowels

There are two basic kinds of phones in any language: vowels and consonants. Vowels are produced when the airstream from the lungs is allowed to pass through the mouth without blockage. Consonants, on the other hand, are produced by a blockage (partial or complete) of the airstream.

Vowels are definable in terms of: (1) the position of the tongue on its vertical axis (high, mid, low), and (2) its position on its horizontal

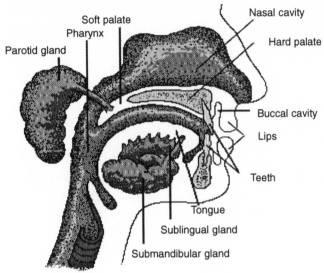

Soft palate
Pharynx
Parotid gland
Nasal cavity
Hard palate
Buccal cavity
Lips
Teeth
Tongue
Sublingual gland
Submandibular gland

FIGURE 3.1
Phonatory Organs

axis (front, central, back). For example, the tongue is moved from low to high in pronouncing the two vowels of *mai*, and from back to front in pronouncing successively the vowel sounds in *tu* and *lì*. The quality of a vowel also depends on whether the speaker keeps the lips rounded or unrounded, the jaws close together or open, or the tip of the tongue flat or curled up *(retroflex)*. These categories allow phoneticians to catalogue all possible vocalic sounds.

In some languages, the vowels take on the nasal quality of any nasal consonant that surrounds them in words. To illustrate, in French the vowel [a] becomes nasalized, shown with the symbol [ã], before a nasal consonant: for example, the word *gant* ('glove') is pronounced [gã]. This nasalization feature of vowels is not found in Italian. If vowels are *stressed* (i.e., if they bear the main accent) they are slightly longer than when they are not stressed. This is shown by adding the diacritic [:] after the vowel phone: for example, [a] represents a short vowel phone, as in *gatto* ('cat'), and [a:] a long one, as in *cane* ('dog'). The transcription of these two words would show this as follows: *gatto* = [ga-t:o]; *cane* = [ka:-ne] ([t:] = double [tt]).

The standard Italian vowel subsystem has seven main phones:

ELEVATION OF TONGUE	DEGREE OF TONGUE RAISING	POINT OF TONGUE ELEVATION			
		Front	Central		Back
			retroflex	flat	rounded
High	close	[i]			[u]
	open	–			–
Mid	close	[e]			[o]
	open	[ɛ]			[ɔ]
Low	close				
	open			[a]	

Since various distinctions are not essential in referring to the Italian vowels – as for instance the retroflex vs. the flat distinction – the articulatory definitions of the seven vowels of Italian can be abridged as follows:

[i] = high front
[u] = high back
[e] = mid-front close
[ɛ] = mid-front open
[o] = mid-back close
[ɔ] = mid-back open
[a] = low central

If more detail in articulatory description is required for studying, say, dialectal vowel variants, then the above chart provides the categories to do so. Note, as well, that each vowel becomes lengthened when it bears the primary stress in an *open syllable* – a syllable that ends in a vowel:

SHORT VOWELS			LONG VOWELS		
[i]	vitto	*food*	[i:]	vino	*wine*
[e]	becco	*beak*	[e:]	bere	*to drink*
[ɛ]	bello	*beautiful*	[ɛ:]	era	*era*
[o]	corto	*brief*	[o:]	come	*how*
[ɔ]	botta	*bang*	[ɔ:]	rosa	*rose*
[a]	gatto	*cat*	[a:]	cane	*dog*

Here are some examples of these vowels as they occur in words. The transcriptions provided include consonant phones and primary stress mark (here we will use the diacritic [´] placed on the stressed vowel):

	SHORT			LONG	
	[a]			[a:]	
acqua	[ák:-wa]	*water*	andare	[an-dá:-re]	*to go*
alto	[ál-to]	*tall*	fare	[fá:-re]	*to do*
	[o]			[o:]	
oggi	[ó-ĵ:i]	*today*	come	[kó:-me]	*how*
occhio	[ó-k:yo]	*eye*	nome	[nó:-me]	*name*
	[ɔ]			[ɔ:]	
osso	[ɔ́-s:o]	*bone*	cosa	[kɔ́:-za]	*thing*
orto	[ɔ́r-to]	*brief*	poco	[pɔ́:-ko]	*few*
	[e]			[e:]	
dentro	[dén-tro]	*inside*	pera	[pé:-ra]	*pear*
mento	[mén-to]	*chin*	spesa	[spé:-za]	*shopping*
	[ɛ]			[ɛ:]	
bello	[bɛ́-l:o]	*beautiful*	era	[ɛ́:-ra]	*era*
vento	[vɛ́n-to]	*wind*	spera	[spɛ́:-ra]	*s/he hopes*
	[i]			[i:]	
finto	[fín-to]	*fake*	filo	[fí:-lo]	*string*
pista	[pís-ta]	*runway*	vino	[ví:-no]	*wine*
	[u]			[u:]	
punta	[pún-ta]	*tip*	uva	[ú:-va]	*grapes*
tutto	[tú-t:o]	*all*	cura	[kú:-ra]	*cure*

The open vowels [ɛ] and [ɔ] occur only in a stressed syllable. In general, however, the distinction between an open or close vowel is one of degree. Historically speaking, this distinction is not a universal one in the language as it is spoken across the Italian peninsula. Moreover, as we shall see below, even in standard Italian, there are various structural factors that constrain and regulate the opening and closing of the mid vowel sounds.

The Consonants

Consonants are phones produced by a blockage of the airstream. As we discussed above, the two aspects of articulation that are relevant to describing and classifying consonants are the point and the manner of articulation. The relevant points of articulation for describing the Italian consonants are:

1. *bilabial* (upper and lower lips)
2. *labiodental* (lower lips and upper teeth)
3. *dental* (upper teeth)
4. *palatal* (hard palate)
5. *velar* (soft palate)

Categories such as *alveolar* (gum ridge), *palato-alveolar* (ridge and palate), and *glottal* (throat) are not necessary for the description of standard Italian consonant phones, although they may be needed to describe regional and dialectal variants of the language.

As for *manner of articulation*, the relevant categories are:

1. *plosive* (complete stoppage of the airstream), also known as *stop* or *occlusive*
2. *fricative* (constriction or turbulence in letting the airstream through the mouth)
3. *affricate* (combination of plosive + fricative articulations)
4. *flap* (tongue flapping in the production of the consonant), also known as *vibrant*
5. *lateral* (narrowing the tongue as the airstream escapes from the sides of the tongue)
6. *nasal* (airstream resonates in the nasal passage).

Some phoneticians prefer to use the term *sibilant* in place of *fricative* to describe consonants that are produced by hissing: e.g. the [s] in *sera* or the [ʃ] in *sciocco*. Flaps and laterals are classified together as *liquids*.

Some consonants can be pronounced with or without the vibration of the vocal cords in the larynx. For example, the difference between the initial sounds of *sip* and *zip* can be easily identified by putting a finger over the throat as they are pronounced: in the pronunciation of *s* no vibration can be felt, while in the pronunciation of *z* a distinct vibration can be felt. The term used to refer to 'nonvibrating consonants' is *voiceless*; that used to refer to 'vibrating consonants' is *voiced*. Nasals, flaps, and laterals are, by their very nature, always voiced. The others have to be classified as either voiceless of voiced.

The symbols that we will use in this book to describe the consonants of standard Italian are charted below (vls = voiceless, vd = voiced):

MANNER		Bilabial	Labiodental	Dental	Palatal	Velar
				POINT		
Plosive	vls	[p]		[t]	[č]	[k]
	vd	[b]		[d]	[ĵ]	[g]
Fricative	vls		[f]	[s]	[ʃ]	
	vd		[v]	[z]	—	
Affricate	vls			[ts]		
	vd			[dz]		
Flap					[r]	
Lateral			[l]	[ļ]	[ʎ]	
Nasal		[m]		[n]	[ń]	[ŋ]

Like the vowels, the Italian consonant phones can now be defined in articulatory terms as follows:

[p] = voiceless bilabial plosive (stop)
[b] = voiced bilabial plosive (stop)
[t] = voiceless dental plosive (stop)
[d] = voiced dental plosive (stop)
[č] = voiceless palatal plosive (stop)
[ĵ] = voiced palatal plosive (stop)
[k] = voiceless velar plosive (stop)
[g] = voiced velar plosive (stop)
[f] = voiceless labiodental fricative
[v] = voiced labiodental fricative
[s] = voiceless dental fricative (sibilant)
[z] = voiced dental fricative (sibilant)
[ʃ] = voiceless palatal fricative (sibilant)
[ts] = voiceless dental affricate
[dz] = voiced dental affricate
[r] = palatal flap (vibrant)
[l] = dental lateral
[ļ] = palatal lateral
[ʎ] = velar lateral
[m] = bilabial nasal
[n] = dental nasal
[ń] = palatal nasal
[ŋ] = velar nasal

There are several things to note with regard to the above classificatory scheme. First, the classification of a sound into a specific category – labiodental, palatal, and so on – does not preclude the fact that it can vary somewhat, from speaker to speaker, and from word to word (for structural reasons). Thus, the dental [t] may be pronounced as more alveodental by some speakers and as almost interdental by others. Again, like the vowels, classifications are really prototypical or 'median' decisions, rather than absolute ones. Second, the laterals [l], [ʎ], [ɫ] and the nasals [n], [ń], [ŋ] are variants of the same basic types of sound. As we shall see in the next chapter, Italian laterals and nasals are influenced by the point of articulation of the following consonant – a process known as *assimilation*: that is, [ʎ] and [ń] are sounds that result from the influence of a following palatal consonant ([č], [ĵ], and [ʃ]), while the velar [ɫ] and [ŋ] result from the influence of a following velar consonant ([k], [g]):

ITALIAN LATERALS

[ʎ] *before a palatal consonant*		[ɫ] *before a velar consonant*		[l] *before any other consonant*	
falce	[fál- če]	falco	[fáɫ -ko]	alto	[ál-to]
Belgio	[bél-ĵo]	colgo	[kóɫ -go]	calmo	[kál-mo]

ITALIAN NASALS

[ń] *before a palatal consonant*		[ŋ] *before a velar consonant*		[n] *before any other consonant*	
pancia	[páń-ča]	anche	[áŋ -ke]	tanto	[tán-to]
mangia	[máń-ĵa]	sangue	[sáŋ-gwe]	vendo	[vén-do]

Here are examples of the other Italian consonant phones as they occur in words:

	[p]				[b]	
pane	[pá:-ne]	*bread*		bene	[bé:-ne]	*well*
palla	[pá-l:a]	*ball*		bravo	[brá-vo]	*good*
	[t]				[d]	
tutto	[tú-t:o]	*all*		dove	[dó:-ve]	*where*
treno	[tré:-no]	*train*		dire	[dí:-re]	*to say*
	[č]				[ĵ]	
cena	[čé:-na]	*dinner*		gioco	[ĵó-ko]	*game, play*
ciao	[čá:-o]	*hi, bye*		gente	[ĵén-te]	*people*

	[k]			[g]	
cane	[ká:-ne]	*dog*	gatto	[gá-t:o]	*cat*
chi	[kí:]	*who*	grande	[grán-de]	*big*

	[f]			[v]	
fare	[fá:-re]	*to do*	vero	[vé:-ro]	*true*
freddo	[fré-d:o]	*cold*	venire	[ve-ní:-re]	*to come*

	[s]			[z]	
sale	[sá:-le]	*salt*	sbaglio	[zbá-λ:o]	*mistake*
sperare	[spe-rá:-re]	*to hope*	snello	[zné-l:o]	*slim*

	[ʃ]			[ts]/[dz]	
scemo	[ʃé:-mo]	*silly*	zio	[tsí:-o]	*uncle*
sciocco	[ʃɔ́-k:o]	*bland*	zero	[dzɛ́-ro]	*zero*

	[r]			[m]	
raro	[rá:-ro]	*rare*	mamma	[má-m:a]	*mother*
rete	[ré:-te]	*net(work)*	mela	[mé:-la]	*apple*

Note that different phonetic symbols for some of the sounds charted above are used in the relevant technical literature and, in the case of palatal [č] and [ĵ], may even be classified in a different category – as affricates rather than as plosives. We will not discuss differences in phonetic conventions here. Knowing the articulatory definition of a sound (as bilabial, plosive, etc.) will allow the user of this book to figure out to what sound the symbol used by phoneticians refers.

Note the following differences between Italian and English consonant phones:

- The English [p] is aspirated, that is, pronounced with a slight puff of air (represented as [pʰ]), when it occurs in word-initial position followed by a vowel (e.g., *pin, pill,* etc.). This aspiration is otherwise blocked (*spin, spill,* etc.). The standard Italian [p] is never aspirated.
- In English the tip of the tongue is raised to touch the alveolar ridge, just behind the upper front teeth, in the articulation of words containing dental plosives, such as *tip* and *dip.* In Italian, the tip of the tongue always touches the upper front teeth. The difference can be heard in the articulation of word pairs such as Italian *treno* vs. English *train* and Italian *drastico* vs. English *drastic.* For this reason, the English plosives are more precisely classified as *alveodental,* and transcribed with the symbols [t̪] and [d̪].

- The Italian affricates [ts] and [dz] are represented in spelling with the letter *z*: for example, *zio* = [tsí:-o], *zero* = [dzé:-ro]. This same letter is used in English to represent [z] instead. The difference can be observed in word pairs such as Italian *zero* vs. English *zero* and Italian *zingaro* vs. English *zing*. The voiceless consonant [ts] is similar to the *ts* in English *cats*, and the voiced one [dz] to the *ds* in *fads*.
- The [s] and [z] are represented by the same alphabet character *s* in Italian. The former is comparable to the *s* in English *sip*, the latter to the *z* in English *zip*, and is not to be confused, as we have just observed, with the affricate pronunciation of the Italian *z* (in words such as *zero* and *zingaro*). As we shall see in the next chapter, [z] occurs before voiced consonants (as in *sbaglio* and *snello*) and between vowels (as in *casa* and *rosa*).
- In English the lateral consonant is 'velarized' ([ɫ]) when it occurs at the end of a syllable or word, as in *kill*, *bill*, and so forth; it is pronounced by raising the back part of the tongue towards the throat. In Italian, on the other hand, the [l] is always dental in this position, as in *quello*, *bello*, and so forth; it is articulated with the tip of the tongue touching the upper teeth.

To conclude the discussion on consonant phones, it is worth mentioning that the categories used above are specific. Phoneticians also employ more general categories that are useful when describing the sounds of the world's languages. Two of the more commonly used ones are the following:

- *Noncontinuants vs. continuants:* The plosive consonants are classified, more generally, as **noncontinuants**, that is, as consonants produced with total obstruction of the airstream; all other consonants (fricatives, liquids, and nasals) are classified instead as **continuants**, because in their articulation the airstream flows continuously from the mouth.
- *Obstruents vs. sonorants:* The plosives, fricatives, and affricates are classified as **obstruents** because in their articulation the airstream cannot escape through the nose and because it is either totally or partially obstructed in its flow through the vocal tract. The **sonorants** are sounds produced with a relatively free flow of air through the vocal or nasal cavities, and thus have greater sonority than obstruents. The vowels and the liquids ([l], [r]), for exam-

ple, are sonorants (i.e., they are produced with a strong vibration of the vocal cords).

The Double Consonants

In general, most of the Italian consonant phones have **double** counterparts, known generally as *geminate consonants*. These do not exist as such in English, even though double letters are often used (to represent single consonants) and double articulations can occur across syllable boundaries – for example, in *bookkeeper* the [k] is essentially a geminate consonant. The Italian double consonants last approximately twice as long as corresponding single ones and are pronounced much more tensely. Double consonants occur between vowels, or after a vowel and before a liquid ([l], [r]).

Double consonants are transcribed in two ways: (1) with the corresponding phone symbol repeated (e.g., [tt], [dd]. etc.), or (2) as with lengthened vowels, with the diacritic [:] (e.g., [t:], [d:], etc.). We will use the latter convention here.

The plosives and affricates have corresponding geminates, as do the fricatives except for [z]. The dental lateral [l] and the nasals [m] and [n] also have corresponding geminates. There are no corresponding double consonants of the velar [ɫ] and [ŋ] phones. The reason for this is structural, as we shall see in the next chapter. There are, however, lateral and nasal geminates: (1) the double palatal nasal sound represented in writing by *gn* (*sogno, bagno,* etc.) is symbolized phonetically by [ń]; (2) the double palatal lateral sound represented in writing by *gli* (*figlio, luglio,* etc.) is symbolized phonetically by [λ]. To show that these are geminate sounds, they are often represented with the diacritic [:]: [ń:], [λ:].

The double consonants of standard Italian are charted below:

MANNER		Bilabial	Labiodental	Dental	Palatal	Velar
Plosive	vls	[p:]		[t:]	[č:]	[k:]
	vd	[b:]		[d:]	[ĵ:]	[g:]
Fricative	vls		[f:]	[s:]	[ʃ:]	
	vd		[v:]	–	–	
Affricate	vls			[ts:]		
	vd			[dz:]		
Flap					[r:]	
Lateral				[l:]	[λ:]	
Nasal		[m:]		[n:]	[ń:]	

Historically, double consonants are a characteristic of central and southern Italian pronunciation. They are generally not a feature of northern Italian dialectal or regional speech, as we shall discuss in Chapter 8. However, recall from the previous two chapters that dialectally based differences are gradually disappearing in Italian today. Here are examples of the double consonants as they occur in words:

	[p:]				[b:]	
troppo	[trɔ́-p:o]	*too much*	conobbe	[ko-nó-b:e]	*s/he knew*
seppe	[sé-p:e]	*s/he knew*	rabbia	[rá-b:ya]	*anger*
	[t:]				[d:]	
tutto	[tú-t:o]	*all*	cadde	[ká-d:e]	*s/he fell*
fatto	[fá-t:o]	*fact*	addurre	[a-d:ú-r:e]	*to add(uce)*
	[č:]				[ĵ:]	
braccio	[brá-č:o]	*arm*	legge	[lé-ĵ:e]	*s/he reads*
faccia	[fá-č:a]	*face*	oggi	[ó-ĵ:i]	*today*
	[k:]				[g:]	
secco	[sé-k:o]	*dry*	leggo	[lé-g:o]	*I read*
occhi	[ó-k:i]	*eyes*	reggono	[ré-g:o-no]	*they hold*
	[f:]				[v:]	
baffi	[bá-f:i]	*moustache*	bevve	[bé-v:e]	*s/he drank*
soffio	[só-f:yo]	*I blow*	davvero	[da-v:é:-ro]	*really*
	[s:]				[ʃ:]	
basso	[bá-s:o]	*short*	lascio	[lá-ʃ:o]	*I leave*
rosso	[ró-s:o]	*red*	ruscello	[ru-ʃ:é-l:o]	*stream*
	[ts:]/[dz:]				[r:]	
razza	[rá-ts:a]	*race*	corro	[kó-r:o]	*I run*
mezzo	[mé-dz:o]	*half*	terra	[té-r:a]	*earth*
	[m:]				[n:]	
mamma	[má-m:a]	*mother*	nonno	[nɔ́-n:o]	*grandfather*
cammino	[ka-m:í:-no]	*I walk*	cenno	[čé-n:o]	*wink*
	[ń]				[λ:]	
sogno	[só-ń:o]	*dream*	figlio	[fí- λ:o]	*son*
giugno	[ĵú-ń:o]	*June*	luglio	[lú- λ:o]	*July*

Syllable Structure

Consonant and vowel phones are called *segments* because they are, literally, the physical segments of sound that make up syllables. A

syllable is a word, or a part of a word, uttered in a single vocal impulse. Syllables are also known as *breath groups* because they allow for the taking in of breath.

The essential component of the syllable is its **nucleus**, which is normally a vowel (and in languages other than Italian sometimes a liquid consonant). This nucleus is always marked by a degree of **stress**, which may be *primary* (also known as *main accent*) or *secondary* and *tertiary* when the syllables are part of a polysyllabic word (a word with many syllables). The diacritic we are using here to indicate primary stress is [´], placed on the syllable (*mela* = [mé:-la]).

Stress is an example of a **nonsegmental** feature (any feature that is not a vowel or consonant). More precisely, it is a **suprasegmental** or *prosodic* feature because it occurs in a 'superimposed' fashion with a vocalic segment (i.e., concomitantly with a vowel). Above we have been showing the end of a syllable with the diacritic [-] (*fare* = [fá:-re], *fatto* = [fá-t:o]), a practice that we will continue to use throughout this book.

Any of the Italian vowels can stand as nucleus of a syllable, and, as we have seen, may be either long or short. The segments that can come before or after a vocalic nucleus are known as **contours**. All single consonants, except the palatal and velar laterals and nasals ([ʎ], [ɫ], [ɲ], [ŋ]) – which, as we saw above, are restricted to occurring before lateral and velar consonants – can be *prenuclear contours* (segments coming before the nuclear vowel). If the syllable ends with the vowel, it is called an **open syllable**; if it ends with a consonant, it is called **closed**. Note that a vowel is long only in a stressed open syllable:

V	=	unstressed syllable consisting of a nuclear vowel (open)
V́:	=	stressed syllable consisting of a nuclear lengthened vowel (open)
CV-	=	unstressed syllable with a prenuclear consonant (open)
CV́:-	=	stressed syllable consisting of a prenuclear consonant (open)
VC-	=	unstressed syllable with a postnuclear consonant (closed)
V́C-	=	stressed syllable with a postnuclear consonant (closed)
CVC-	=	unstressed syllable with a pre- and postnuclear consonants (closed)
CV́C-	=	stressed syllable with a pre- and postnuclear consonants (closed)

UNSTRESSED				STRESSED			
V	CV-	VC-	CVC-	V́:	CV́:-	V́C-	CV́C-
a lui	magari	andò	mandò	ho	mano	anche	manca
[a]	[ma-ga:-ri]	[an-dó:]	[man-dó:]	[o:]	[má:-no]	[áŋ-ke]	[máŋ-ka]
e io	diritto	saltò	cartone	ha	vero	alto	calza
[e]	[di-rí-t:o]	[sal-tó:]	[kar-tó:-ne]	[a:]	[vé:-ro]	[ál-to]	[kál-tsa]

Note that if the second postnuclear consonant in the sequence CVCC is a liquid, then the previous syllable is open: *vedrò* = [ve-dró:], *duplicare* = [du-pli-ká:-re]. Prenuclear two-consonant clusters are also found in Italian: C_1C_2V (the numerical subscripts indicate that the consonants are different). But the consonants that can be combined in the C_1C_2 cluster are limited by certain rules. Only if the first consonant is [s] or [z] before voiced consonants (C_1 = [s], [z]), can C_2 be most any other consonant (C_2 = [p, b, t, d, ...]): for example, *spero, stufo, sfera, sbaglio*. Another common prenuclear cluster is one in which the second consonant is a flap (C_2 = [r]): for example, *primo, grande, troppo*. Three-consonant clusters ($C_1C_2C_3$) are infrequent, and the first consonant C_1 must normally be [s] and the C_3 [r]: for example, *sprecare, sdraiarsi*.

Double consonants (C:) cannot occur in word-initial position and must follow a vowel: for example, *fatto, troppo*. The vowel that precedes a double consonant is always short, even in a stressed syllable: *fatto* = [fá-t:o], *bello* = [bé-l:o].

Vocalic sounds may also be nuclear contours. If the vowel comes before the nucleus, then it is called a *semiconsonant glide* and the syllable is called a *rising diphthong*, because the stress pattern of the syllable starts with the glide and peaks at the vocalic nucleus: for example, the first syllable of *ieri* is a rising diphthong because the voice pitch is raised as it moves from the glide to the vowel. A *diphthong* is, in effect, a blend of two vowel sounds in one syllable. The rising diphthong consists of a modified articulation of [i] or [u] as the prenuclear contours, each becoming a glide sound – respectively [y] and [w] – pronounced with more tension, hence the designation *semiconsonant*. This type of sound can be represented with S_1 – the subscript indicates that it is the first element in the syllable. A rising diphthong can occur in an open (stressed or unstressed) syllable, S_1V-, or a closed syllable, S_1VC. Needless to say, the V in this syllable structure cannot be the same as the semiconsonant: that is, if S_1 = [y], then the V cannot be [i]; similarly if the S_1 = [w], then the V cannot be [u]. Here are some examples of rising diphthongs:

UNSTRESSED		STRESSED	
S_1 = [y]	S_1 = [w]	S_1 = [y]	S_1 = [w]
fienile	questura	ieri	questo
[fye-ní:-le]	[kwes-tú:-ra]	[yé:-ri]	[kwés-to]
fiumicino	puerile	chiosco	cuoco
[fyu-mi-í:-no]	[pwe-rí:-le]	[kyós-ko]	[kwɔ́:-ko]

A *falling diphthong* is a syllable consisting of a postnuclear vowel. In this case the glide sound of the vocalic contour is less tense and is thus called, more appropriately, a *semivowel* (S_2). To distinguish the semiconsonantal glides [y] and [w] from the semivocalic ones, the symbols [i̯] and [u̯] respectively are sometimes used for the latter. In a falling diphthong the stress pattern of the syllable starts with the vocalic nucleus, falling towards the semivowel: for example, the first syllable of *causa* is a falling diphthong because the voice pitch falls as it moves from the nuclear [a] to the semivowel [u̯]. A falling diphthong is, by its very nature, a closed syllable structure, (C)VS_2, and the nuclear vowel, as a consequence, always short. Falling diphthongs are rather infrequent in Italian:

UNSTRESSED		STRESSED	
S_2 = [i̯]	S_2 = [u̯]	S_2 = [i̯]	S_2 = [u̯]
deificare	cautela	mai	causa
[dei̯-fi-ká:re]	[kau̯-té:-la]	[mái̯]	[káu̯-za]
mainate	pausare	sei (six)	pausa
[mai̯-ná:-te]	[pau̯-zá:-re]	[séi̯]	[páu̯-za]

Syllables consisting of a prenuclear semiconsonant and a postnuclear semivowel (S_1VS_2), which are rare, are called *triphthongs*. These have a rise-peak-fall pattern: *miei* = [myέi̯], *suoi* = [swói̯], *quei* = [kwέi̯], and so on.

If two adjacent vowels belong to different syllables, then no diphthong or triphthong is formed. There is, instead, a slight pause between the vowels, known as a *hiatus*: for example, *paura* = [pa-ú:-ra], *farmacia* = [far-ma-čí:-a].

Italian *phonetic syllabication*, or the division of words into syllables, has been explained by illustration above. This is different from the conventional syllabication of written words. Phonetic syllabication is based, as we have seen, on syllabic structure, not on orthographic conventions. For example, the practice in writing is to separate double consonants, whereas phonetically the double consonant is considered to be a phonic unit belonging to its own syllable: *fatto* = *fat-to* = [fá-t:o]. Nevertheless, some linguists prefer to use the double symbol to indicate syllabic structure as follows: [fát-to].

Prenuclear contours, consonantal or semiconsonantal, are generally classified under the rubric of **onset**, and postnuclear ones under **coda**. Note that in rhyming words, the nucleus + coda of the final syllable must match: *via* – *mia*, *spreco* – *greco*, and so on. For this reason, the nucleus + coda sequence constitutes a more general category known as a *rhyme*. This approach to the syllable makes it possible to show its *hierarchical structure* more precisely. For example, the monosyllabic word *spreco* has the following structure:

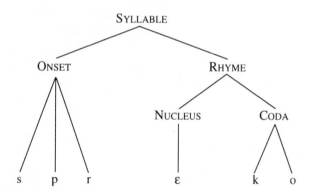

Prosodic Features

The main prosodic, or nonsegmental, features studied by phoneticians include: stress, tone, and intonation. As we have seen above, in every word there is a stressed syllable – the one that carries the main accent. We have shown this by using the diacritic ['] before the syllable.

Phonetically, the term *stress* refers to the fact that a syllable is articulated louder and more strongly than others in a word or in a sentence. The actual quantity of stress given to a syllable does not matter; it is the relative amount given to each that is of relevance. In polysyllabic words, there is one main, or *primary*, stress, a *secondary* stress, and a *tertiary* or *unstressed* syllable. There are two ways to show differences among the three types of stress: (1) with numerals before the syllable – [^{1}] = primary stress, [^{2}] = secondary stress, [^{3}] = tertiary stress; (2) with accent marks on the nuclear vowel – [ˊ] = primary stress, [ˋ] = secondary stress, [ ] (nothing) = tertiary stress. For example, in the word *aprire* = [a-prí:-re], the second syllable bears the primary stress, the first secondary, and the third tertiary. This can be shown as [^{2}a-^{1}pri:-^{3}re] or [à-prí-re].

Stress is part of rhythmic patterns in language and it has an internal hierarchical structure. Using a tree diagram, we can show how, for instance, the word *disfatto* is really *dis* + *fatto*, with *fatto* retaining its original stress pattern (S = strong or primary stress, W = weak or secondary stress):

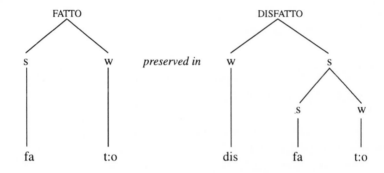

This way of showing stress pattern makes it possible to indicate how a syllable may be considered to be a subportion of a larger unit, sometimes called a *foot*. This method shows, in other words, that stress pattern has a *metrical structure*.

Most two-syllable words in Italian are stressed on the next-to-last syllable: *fatto* = [fá-t:o], *mano* = [má:-no], *pasta* = [pás-ta]. Words consisting of more than two syllables are generally stressed on the next-to-last syllable as well: *amico* = [a-mí:-ko], *appuntamento* = [a-p:un-ta-mén-to], *gelato* = [ǰe-lá:-to]. However, there are a number of exceptions to this general rule, which constitute the source of many errors in stress allocation among students of Italian: *automobile* = [au̯-to-mó:-bi-le], *facile* = [fá-či-le], *lampada* = [lám-pa-da].

In some words, the stress falls on the last syllable. In written form, there is always an accent mark in such words, usually grave (ˋ), on the final vowel: *caffè* = [ka-f:é], *città* = [či-t:á], *abilità* = [a-bi-li-tá].

In addition to word stress, phoneticians also study *sentence stress* patterns. When words are combined into sentences, only one word generally bears the main stress. Exceptions to this rule are those sentences that require emphasis or contrast. In simple Italian statements and questions, the main stress is normally placed on the last word:

> *Maria è italiana*
> *Mio cugino arriva domani*
> *Come si chiama?*
> *Dove sei andata ieri?*

Simple sentences such as these can, of course, be spoken with a different stress pattern to highlight different words:

> *Maria è italiana (non lui)*
> *Mio cugino arriva domani (non mia cugina)*
> etc.

If words of the same kind (all nouns, all adjectives, etc.) occur in a series, then each one is stressed:

> *Qui si vendono camicie, pantaloni e scarpe*
> *Claudia sa pattinare, sciare e nuotare*
> *Preferisci tè o caffè?*

In sentences consisting of more than one clause, the final word of both clauses is generally stressed, unless some other word is to be emphasized:

> *Parlate molto, ma non sapete quello che dite*
> *Lei è molto intelligente, ma è un po' ingenua*

Tone is defined as the relative height of pitch with which a syllable, a word, and so forth is pronounced. The use of tonal distinction is not as critical in Italian as it is, for instance, in North Mandarin Chinese, in which numerous words are distinguished by differences in the rise and fall of tone. The single syllable [ma], for example, can have various meanings according to whether the tone is level (—), rising (↑), dipping (↕) or falling (↓):

[ma —] = *mother*
[ma ↑] = *hemp*
[ma ↕] = *horse*
[ma ↓] = *scold*

In Italian, tone is used not to distinguish the meaning of words, but to signal differences in type of sentence. This is known as **intonation**. Italian statements, for instance, end with a falling intonation pattern:

Maria è francese (↓)
Mio cugino arriva domani (↓)

The same intonation pattern applies to questions that require an answer beyond a *yes* or a *no,* which always start with interrogative words (*chi, quando,* etc.):

Come ti chiami? (↓)
Dove abiti? (↓)
etc.

On the other hand, Italian questions that can be answered with a *yes* or a *no* end with a rising intonation pattern:

Parla italiano Lei? (↑)
Conosce la signora Bertini? (↑)
etc.

This intonation pattern applies as well to *tag* questions, which are brief questions 'tagged on' to the end of sentences:

Giovanni è italiano, non è vero? (↑)
Tu conosci Claudio, no? (↑)
etc.

If a statement or question involves words in a series, then the rising intonation pattern is used with each choice, except the last one, in which case it falls:

Parlo bene l'italiano, (↑) *il tedesco* (↑) *e il giapponese* (↓)

Vuoi andare al cinema, (↑) al teatro (↑) o alla discoteca? (↓)
Maria è intelligente, (↑) ricca (↑) e bella (↓)

Orthography

As we mentioned at the start of this chapter, linguists have developed a *phonetic alphabet* because the spelling, or *orthographic*, system of a language is generally unreliable. Although alphabetic writing is basically phonetic, no alphabet perfectly represents a language. This is because pronunciations vary over time, and they also vary geographically; but these are not always reflected in changes to the orthographic system. In English, for example, the *k* in *knife, knave, knot,* and so on no longer represents a velar plosive, because such a consonant disappeared before a nasal at a certain point several hundred years ago. However, the orthographic spelling has never been changed to reflect this phonetic change.

The Italian alphabet has the following characters (the foreign characters are noted with an asterisk):

LETTER	NAME	EXAMPLE	ENGLISH
a, A	a	amico	*friend*
b, B	bi	bene	*well*
c, C	ci	casa	*house*
		ciao	*hi/bye*
		che	*what*
		cena	*dinner*
d, D	di	dopo	*after*
e, E	e	età	*age*
f, F	effe	figlia	*daughter*
g, G	gi	gatto	*cat*
		gelo	*frost*
		ghetto	*ghetto*
		giorno	*day*
h, H	acca (always silent)	ho	*I have*
i, I	i	italiano	*Italian*
j, J (*)	i lunga	jazz	*jazz*
k, K (*)	cappa	karatè	*karate*
l, L	elle	lira	*lira*
m, M	emme	mano	*hand*
n, N	enne	nonno	*grandfather*
o, O	o	ora	*now*

p, P	pi	pane	*bread*
q, Q	cu	quando	*when*
r, R	erre	rosso	*red*
s, S	esse	sempre	*always*
t, T	ti	tanto	*a lot*
u, U	u	uva	*grapes*
v, V	vu/vi	vero	*true*
w, W (*)	doppia vu	weekend	*weekend*
x, X (*)	ics	xenofobia	*xenophobia*
y, Y (*)	ipsilon, i greca	yogurt	*yogurt*
z, Z	zeta	zucchero	*sugar*

Generally speaking, Italian orthography is highly phonetic: that is, each one of its letters, known as *graphs*, stands generally for one sound. There are, however, some exceptions to this rule:

- The graph *i* stands for the vowel [i], the semiconsonant [y], and the semivowel [i̯]: *pino* = [pí:-no], *pieno* = [pyέ:-no], *mai* = [mái̯].
- Similarly, the graph *u* stands for [u], [w], and [u̯]: *uva* = [ú:-va], *uomo* + [wɔ́:-mo], *causa* = [káu̯-za].
- The graphs *e* and *o* stand for both open and close vowels: *beve* = [bé:-ve], *bela* = [bέ:-la], *come* = [kó:-me], *ora* = [ɔ́:-ra]
- Except for an accented final vowel (*caffè, città*), stress patterns are not indicated in Italian orthography.
- The *digraph* (a combination of two letters representing one sound) *gn* stands for [ń], and the *trigraph* (a combination of three letters representing one sound) *gli* stands for [λ:]: *sogno* = [só-ń:o], [*figlio* = [fí-λ:o]. Note, however, that the digraph *gl* can also stand for the cluster [gl]: *glicerina* = [gli-če-rí:-na], *globo* = [glɔ́:-bo], and so forth.
- The letter *c* represents velar [k] before *a, o, u,* or any consonant; it represents palatal [č] before *e, i: cane* = [ká:-ne], *come* = [kó:-me], *cuore* = [kwɔ́:-re], *croce* = [krɔ́:-če], *cena* = [čé:-na], *città* = [či-t:á].
- The digraph *ch* represents velar [k] before *e, i: che* = [ké:], *chiesa* = [kyé:-za]. The digraph *ci* represents palatal [č] before *a, o, u: ciao* = [čá:-o], *bacio* = [bá:-čo], *ciurma* = [čúr-ma].
- The letter *q* always stands for [k] in the sequence *qu: questo* = [kwés-to], *quale* = [kwá:le], etc.
- The letter *g* represents velar [g] before *a, o, u,* or a consonant; it

represents the palatal [ĵ] before *e, i: gatto* = [gá-t:o], *guerra* =
[gwέ-r:a], *grande* = [grán-de], *gelo* = [ĵέ-lo], *giro* = [ĵí:-ro], and so
forth.

- The digraph *gh* represents velar [g] before *e, i: ghetto* = [gé-t:o],
  laghi = [lá:-gi]. The digraph *gi* represents palatal [ĵ] before *a, o, u:*
  giallo = [ĵá-l:o], *giorno* = [ĵórno], *giubba* = [ĵú:-b:a].

- The sequence *sc* represents the phonic cluster [sk] before *a, o, u,* or
  any consonant: *scarpa* = [skár-pa], *scopa* = [skó:-pa], *scuola* =
  [skwó:-la]. It represents [ʃ] and [ʃ:] instead before *e, i: scemo* =
  [ʃé:-mo], *ascesa* = [a-ʃ:é:-za].

- The trigraph *sch* represents the cluster [sk] before the vowels *e i:*
  scherzo = [skέr-tso], *schiena* = [skyé:-na]; the trigraph *sci* represents palatal [ʃ] or [ʃ:] before *a, o, u: sciabola* = [ʃá:-bo-la], *sciocco*
  = [ʃ5:-k:o], *lascia* = [lá-ʃ:a].

- Words spelled with *j, k, w, x,* and *y* are foreign words.

- The letter *h* is used only in several present indicative tense forms
  of the verb *avere: io ho, tu hai, lui/lei ha, loro hanno.* It is always
  silent.

- Capital letters are used at the beginning of sentences and with
  proper nouns. However, unlike English, the following are not capi-
  talized: the pronoun *io*; professional titles; adjectives and nouns referring to language and nationalities (*italiano, francese, inglese,
  spagnolo,* etc.); names of the seasons (*inverno, autunno, primav-
  era, estate*); months of the year (*gennaio, febbraio, marzo, aprile,*
  etc.); and days of the week (*lunedì, martedì, mercoledì, giovedì,*
  etc.).

- The letters *cc, cch, cci, gg, ggh,* and *ggi* represent double articulations of palatal and velar plosives: *bocca, ricci, occhi, leggo,* and
  so forth.

- The digraph *cq* represents the double consonant [k:] in words such
  as *acqua* = [á-k:wa].

- The letter *s* stands for two sounds: voiced [z] before voiced consonants (*sbaglio* = [zbá-λ:o]) and between vowels (*casa* = [ká:-za]);
  and voiceless [s] in all other phonetic environments (*santo* = [sán-
  to], *spero* = [spέ:-ro], etc.).

- The Italian letter *z* represents both [ts] and [dz]: *zio* = [tsí:-o], *zero*
  = [dzέ:-ro]. It is not to be confused with the pronunciation [z] as is
  the corresponding English *z*.

Follow-Up Activities

1. Give reasons why an unambiguous and consistent method of representing the sounds of a language is required in order to describe the language scientifically.

2. Into what areas does the study of sound systems fall?

3. What is the goal of phonetic description?

4. Define the following terms:

   phonetics
   articulatory phonetics
   acoustic phonetics
   point of articulation
   manner of articulation
   vowel
   consonant
   noncontinuant
   continuant
   obstruent
   sonorant
   double consonant
   syllable
   nucleus
   stress
   nonsegmental feature
   suprasegmental feature
   contour
   open syllable
   closed syllable
   onset
   coda
   intonation

5. List the movable and stationary organs of articulation.

6. List the Italian vowel phones and define them in articulatory terms.

Example: [i] = high front vowel

7. Write the phonetic symbol for the stressed vowel in each of the
   following words. Look up any word that you do not know.

   Example: caro = [aː]

   pancia
   vento
   venti
   sera
   serra
   otto
   simpatico
   bocca
   opera
   corpo
   ora
   fine
   io
   luce
   uva

8. List the Italian consonant phones and define them in articulatory
   terms.

   Example: [p] = voiceless bilabial plosive (stop, occlusive)

9. Write the phonetic symbol for the italicized letter(s) in each of the
   following words.

   Example: ca*r*o = [r]

   pa*n*cia
   pa*n*taloni
   a*n*cora
   ca*l*cio
   pa*l*coscenico
   ra*r*o

*a*lto
*l*atte
*sc*emo
ro*b*a
*c*ena
*g*eloso
*c*uore
*g*ola
*f*amiglia
*v*uoto
sa*n*to
*s*pecchio
*s*nello
co*s*a
*s*velare
*t*reno
*z*ucchero
*z*uppa
*s*baglio
va*s*to

10. Write the phonetic symbol for the double consonant in each of the
    following words. Look up any word that you do not know.

    Example: conobbe = [b:]/[bb]

    tutto
    bello
    troppo
    figlia
    giugno
    pesce
    torre
    mamma
    nonno
    baffi
    pezzo
    mezzo
    fosse

leggo
leggi
faccio
becco

11. Transcribe each word phonetically. Look up any word that you do
    not know.

    Example: amici = [a-mí:-či]

    amicizia
    specchio
    palcoscenico
    ragazzo
    ingegno
    cogliere
    lasciare
    correggere
    azzeccare
    imbrogliare
    pancia
    panca
    inchiostro
    miei
    tuoi
    aiuola
    fierezza
    occhio
    acciaio
    stivale
    smesso
    bacio

12. List all the different kinds of syllables and syllable structures.

13. Transcribe the diphthongs and triphthongs in the following words.

    Example: buono = [wo:]

chiesto
quanto
piazza
piuma
chiosco
uomo
quello
mai
sei
pausa
suoi
vuoi
miei
cucchiai

14. Using tree diagrams show the stress patterns of the following
    words. Look up any word which you do not know.

    Example: rosso

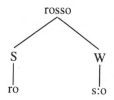

    rossore
    corretto
    correttezza
    errore
    erroneo
    fresco
    rinfresco

15. Show the stress pattern of each word using numerical super-
    scripts. Look up any word that you do not know.

    Example: amico = [^{2}a-^{1}mi:-^{3}ko]

    lampada
    mangiano

amicizia
freddezza
favorire
abilità
simpatico

16. Show the stress and intonation pattern of each sentence. Look up
   any word that you do not know.

   Example: La mia amica è italiana = *La mia am*i*ca è italiana* (↓)

   L'Italia è una penisola che ha la forma di uno stivale.
   Anche due grandi isole sono italiane: la Sicilia e la Sardegna.
   Le catene di montagne principali d'Italia sono le Alpi e gli Ap-
   pennini.
   È vero che i suoi fiumi principali sono il Po, il Tevere e l'Arno?
   Quali sono i mari principali che circondano l'Italia?
   Sono il Mediterraneo e l'Adriatico.
   L'Italia è divisa in venti regioni, vero?
   La capitale d'Italia è Roma, no?
   Tra le sue molte città famose sono da menzionare Firenze,
   Venezia, Milano, Torino, Napoli e Palermo.

17. Transcribe each sentence completely, segmentally, and prosodi-
   cally. Look up any word that you do not know.

   Example: Marco è italiano = [²mar-³ko-¹ɛ:-³i-³ta-²lya:-³no]

   L'Italia è acclamata a livello internazionale per la sua industria
   della moda.
   Tra i suoi stilisti più conosciuti ci sono: Armani, Gucci, Spagnoli,
   Fendi, Inghirami, Valentino, Brioni, Ferragamo, Missoni e altri.
   In generale, gli italiani comprano i loro abiti sia in negozi che in
   magazzini.
   I magazzini principali sono l'Upim e la Standa.
   La macchina che quasi tutti gli italiani guidano è la FIAT, le sue
   lettere stanno per 'Fabbrica Italiana di Automobili di Torino.'

Tra le cosiddette macchine di lusso ci sono la Ferrari, l'Alfa Romeo, la Maserati e la Lancia.

18. Indicate what phone(s) each graph, digraph, or trigraph stands for, writing a word or words that exemplify the different representations.

Example: gn = [ɲ:] – *sogno*

i
u
e
o
c
ch
ci
g
gh
gi
s
sc
sch
sci
z
gn
gli

4

The Italian Sound System

....

A linguistic system is a series of differences of sound combined with a series of differences of ideas.

Ferdinand de Saussure (1857–1913)

Recall, from the previous chapter, that we described the nasal phones [n], [ń], [ŋ] as variants of the same basic type of sound. This sound can be called, for the sake of convenience, 'a prototypical nasal,' and can be identified with slanted lines to distinguish it from any one of its variants: /n/. Each of the three variants, as we also mentioned, was the result of particular environmental (positional) conditions that influenced the actual pronunciation of /n/ as dental [n], palatal [ń], or velar [ŋ]:

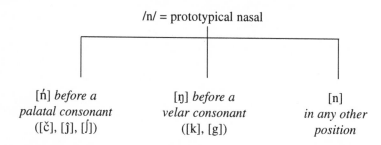

/n/ = prototypical nasal

[ń] *before a*	[ŋ] *before a*	[n]
palatal consonant	*velar consonant*	*in any other*
([č], [ĵ], [ʃ])	([k], [g])	*position*

Here are some examples that clearly show this 'conditioned variation':

• /n/ before palatal consonants is pronounced as [ń]

pancia	=	[páń-ča]
mangia	=	[máń-ĵa]
conscio	=	[kóń-ʃo]

- /n/ before velar consonants is pronounced as [ŋ]:

anche	=	[áŋ-ke]
sangue	=	[sáŋ-gwe]

- /n/ before other consonants is pronounced as [n]:

sento	=	[sén-to]
mando	=	[mán-do]

- /n/ in word-initial position is also pronounced as [n]:

nove	=	[nɔ́:-ve]
nonno	=	[nɔ́-n:o]

- /n/ in word-final position is also pronounced as [n]:

con	=	[kón]
non	=	[nón]

- /n/ between vowels is also pronounced as [n]:

cane	=	[ká:-ne]
pane	=	[pá:-ne]

As these examples show, the ways in which sounds are distributed in actual words make it evident that they are related to each other in patterned or systematic ways. The objective of this chapter is to look precisely at these ways. This falls under the rubric of *phonological analysis*, the component of linguistic method that deals with the patterns that govern pronunciation in a language.

The Phoneme

The /n/ is called, more technically, a **phoneme**. The phonemes of a particular language are those minimal units of sound that can distinguish the meaning of different words in that language. The choice of dental [n] as the symbol to stand for the phoneme, rather than the palatal [ń] or the velar [ŋ], is due to the fact that, as we saw above, it occurs in more environments and, thus, is more prototypical than the other two.

Not all languages share the same repertoire of phonemes. What may be phonemic in one language is not necessarily the case in another. Two different sounds, reflecting distinct articulatory activities, may represent two phonemes in one language but only a single phoneme in another. Take, for instance, [s] and [z]. In English they are phonemic, /s/ and /z/, because they distinguish meaning in such word pairs as: *sip – zip, sing – zing*, and so on. But in Italian, no such pairs exist. As we saw in the previous chapter, the phone [z] occurs before voiced consonants (*sbaglio* = [zbá-λ:o]) and between vowels (*casa* = [ká:-za]), and the voiceless phone [s] in all other positional environments (*specchio* = [spé-k:yo], *suo* = [sú:-o], etc.). These two phones are, therefore, 'environmentally conditioned variants' of a single phoneme, /s/.

Two sounds are identifiable as phonemic, therefore, if they contrast in minimal pairs (*sip – zip, sing – zing*, etc.). A **minimal pair** consists of two words that are identical in composition except for one sound segment that occurs in the same position. Using minimal pairs to determine if two sounds signal a change in meaning, is called the **commutation test**. In this test the '~' symbol is shorthand for 'is commuted with':

/s/ ~ /z/
/s/ is commuted with /z/ in pairs such as:
sip – zip
fuss – fuzz
sing – zing

/s/ ~ /l/
/s/ is commuted with /l/ in pairs such as:
sip – lip
sight – light
song – long

/s/ ~ /r/
/s/ is commuted with /r/ in pairs such as:
sip – rip
sat – rat
sing – ring

etc.

Now, since no minimal pair can be found in Italian to show a **contrast** between [s] and [z], we can now safely conclude that these two phones are variants of the same phoneme, /s/:

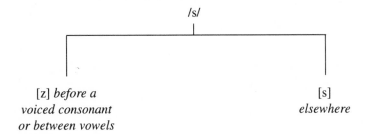

/s/

[z] *before a*
voiced consonant
or between vowels

[s]
elsewhere

Sometimes, two phonemes that can be shown to be in contrast in certain minimal pairs will not be contrastive in others. In English, for example, the vowels /i/ and /ɛ/ are phonemic in pairs such as *beet – bet* = /bit/ ~ /bɛt/. However, some speakers pronounce the word *economics* with an initial [i], others with an initial [ɛ]. When this happens, the two sounds are said to be in **free variation**. This is a rare phenomenon, however, and is usually a consequence of regionally based variation in a language.

Phonemic distinctions are perceived by the hearing centre of the brain and produced through its motor pathways via a complex system of coordination between brain and vocal organs. There are twelve cranial nerves. Seven of these link the brain with the vocal organs. Some perform a motor function, controlling the movement of muscles, while others perform a sensory function, sending signals to the brain. The production of phonemes has its neurophysiological locus in the left hemisphere (LH) of the brain. This discovery goes back to 1861, when the French anthropologist and surgeon Paul Broca noticed a destructive lesion in the left frontal lobe during the autopsy of a patient who had lost the ability to articulate words during his lifetime, even though he had not suffered any paralysis of his speech organs. Broca concluded that the capacity to articulate speech was traceable to that specific cerebral site, which shortly thereafter came to bear his name, *Broca's area*. The role of Broca's area in the production of phonemes was confirmed during the 1950s and 1960s by widely publicized studies conducted by the American psychologist Roger Sperry and his associates. Then, in 1967, the linguist Eric Lenneberg established that the LH was indeed the seat of language, adding that the 'critical period' for language to

'settle into' that hemisphere was from birth to about puberty. The use
of positron emission tomography (PET brain scanning) today in mapping the functions of the brain has confirmed, once and for all, that
Broca's area is where phonemic distinctions originate.

Allophones

The variants of the phoneme /n/ are known more technically as **allophones**. Each allophone, as we have seen, occurs in a predictable environment or set of environments. They are thus said to complement
each other in how they are distributed among the other sounds in the
pronunciation of words. Thus the way they relate to each other structurally is called, logically, **complementary distribution**.

It is the convention in linguistics to take one variant as more basic
than the others and then to state the conditions under which any variation occurs. We chose the dental variant [n] because it occurs in more
environments than the other two phones. Choosing the phone that occurs 'elsewhere' to represent the phoneme is a standard procedure.

The complementary distribution of the allophones of /n/ can now be
stated more formally as follows:

> *The phoneme* /n/ *is realized as palatal* [ń] *before palatal consonants* [č],
> [ʝ], [ʃ], *and as velar* [ŋ] *before velar consonants* [k], [g], *and as dental* [n]
> *in all other phonetic environments.*

For linguists, such a verbal statement is too cumbersome. So, they
prefer to abbreviate it as follows:

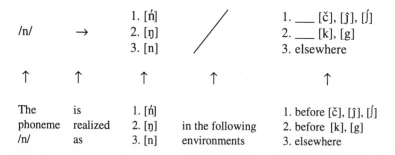

This is called a **phonological rule**, because it shows in a precise and
'economical' fashion the complementary distribution of the allophones

of /n/. Phonological rules are useful devices for showing how the sounds of a language form distributional patterns.

Phonological Analysis

Three tasks are involved in conducting an analysis of sound systems: (1) determining which contrasts are phonemic by means of the commutation test; (2) establishing which allophones belong to which phonemes; (3) formulating appropriate complementary distribution rules. In the case of the vowels, it can be easily established that /a/, /i/, and /u/ are phonemic in Italian from minimal pairs such as the following:

/a/ ~ /i/
ara – ira
pasta – pista

/a/ ~ /u/
arto – urto
basta – busta

/i/ ~ /u/
fine – fune
sì – su

The open and close distinction that pertains to the mid vowels is contrastive only in a few areas of Italy, especially Tuscany. So, the symbols /e/ and /o/ can be chosen as representative of the mid vowel phonemes, regardless of whether they are open or close in their actual articulation:

/e/ ~ /a/
era – ara
pesto – pasto

/e/ ~ /i/
era – ira
che – chi

/e/ ~ /u/
lei – lui
sento – sunto

/o/ ~ /a/
ora – ara
posto – pasto

/o/ ~ /i/
ora – ira
posta – pista

/o/ ~ /u/
orto – urto
pozzo – puzzo

The prenuclear semiconsonants [y] and [w] and the postnuclear semivowels [i̯] and [u̯] described in the previous chapter are allophonic variants of /i/ and /u/: that is, they are glide articulations that occur in predictable syllabic environments. The appropriate complementary distribution rule can be stated as follows:

> *The semiconsonants* [y] and [w] *occur before a nuclear vowel as contours,*
> *and the semivowels* [i̯] *and* [u̯] *after a nuclear vowel.*

This statement can now be expressed as two phonological rules (- = beginning of syllable, V = nuclear vowel):

Rule 1

$$/i/ \quad \rightarrow \quad \begin{bmatrix} [y] / \text{-}\_\_V \\ [i̯] / \text{-}V\_\_ \end{bmatrix}$$

Rule 2

$$/u/ \quad \rightarrow \quad \begin{bmatrix} [w] / \text{-}\_\_V \\ [u̯] / \text{-}V\_\_ \end{bmatrix}$$

Except for the dental fricatives, the laterals, and the nasals, the consonant sounds described in the previous chapter all have phonemic status in Italian. Here is a sampling of minimal pairs that show this:

/p/ ~ /b/
*p*alla – *b*alla

/t/ ~ /d
*t*opo – *d*opo

/d/ ~ /b/
*d*ue – *b*ue

/č/ ~ /ĵ/
*ci*elo – *g*elo

/ĵ/ ~ /g/
*gi*usto – *g*usto

/k/ ~ /p/
*c*ane – *p*ane

/g/ ~ /f/
*g*atto – *f*atto

/f/ ~ /p/
*f*alco – *p*alco

/v/ ~ /p/
*v*ino – *p*ino

/ʃ/ ~ /t/
con*sci*o – con*t*o

/r/ ~ /k/
*r*aro – *c*aro

/m/ ~ /ts/
*m*io – *z*io

The affricates /ts/ and /dz/ are in free variation: that is, the use of one or the other in many words may vary according to the region from which the speaker comes, but it is never distinctive. Now, it can be es-

tablished that /s/, /l/, and /n/ have phonemic status, no matter what their
allophonic realizations are in the following pairs:

/s/ ~ /t/
*s*anto – *t*anto (= [s] allophone)

/s/ ~ /r/
ca*s*a – ca*r*a (= [z] allophone)

/l/ ~ /m/
*l*ira – *m*ira (= [l] allophone)

/l/ ~ /r/
pa*l*chi – pa*r*chi (=[ɫ] allophone)

/n/ ~ /v/
*n*ero – *v*ero (= [n] allophone)

/n/ ~ /r/
pu*n*go – pu*r*go (= [ŋ] allophone)

The phoneme /s/, as we discussed above, is pronounced as either
voiced [z] or voiceless [s] in a predictable manner: [z] occurs before a
voiced consonant ([b], [d], [ʝ], [g], [v], [r], [l], [m], [n]) and between
vowels; [s] occurs in all other environments:

DISTRIBUTION OF THE ALLOPHONES OF /s/

[z] *before a* *voiced consonant*	[z] *between vowels*	[s] *elsewhere*
sbaglio [zbá-λːo]	*casa* [ká:-za]	*stanco* [stáŋ-ko]
smetto [zmέ-tːo]	*rosa* [rɔ́:-za]	*sempre* [sέm-pre]
slitto [zlí-tːo]	*peso* [pé:-zo]	*spendo* [spέn-do]

The voicing of /s/ before voiced consonants is known as **assimilation**. This is the process whereby a phoneme takes on a phonic property (or properties) of the segment that follows it. The above complementary distribution pattern can thus be put into rule form as follows
(C [+voice] = any voiced consonant):

$$/s/ \quad \rightarrow \quad \begin{bmatrix} [z] \ / \ \_\_ \ C \ [+voice] \\ [z] \ / \ V \ \_\_ \ V \\ [s] \ / \ elsewhere \end{bmatrix}$$

The pronunciation of /l/, as we saw in the previous chapter, is conditioned by its position before certain consonants as follows:

DISTRIBUTION OF THE ALLOPHONES OF /l/

[ʎ] *before a palatal consonant*	[ɫ] *before a velar consonant*	[l] *elsewhere*
falce [fál-če]	*falco* [fáɫ -ko]	*alto* [ál-to]
Belgio [bɛ́l-ĵo]	*colgo* [kɔ́ɫ -go]	*calmo* [kál-mo]
calcio [kál-čo]	*volgo* [vgɫ -go]	*latte* [lá-t:e]

The palatalization and velarization of /l/ before palatals and velars is another instance of assimilation. The complementary distribution of this phoneme can now be formalized as follows (C [+palatal] = any palatal consonant, C [+ velar] = any velar consonant):

$$/l/ \quad \rightarrow \quad \begin{bmatrix} [ʎ] \ / \ \_\_ \ C \ [+palatal] \\ [ɫ] \ / \ \_\_ \ C \ [+velar] \\ [l] \ / \ elsewhere \end{bmatrix}$$

The allophones of /n/, as we have seen, are distributed in the same way:

DISTRIBUTION OF THE ALLOPHONES OF /n/

[ń] *before a palatal consonant*	[ŋ] *before a velar consonant*	[n] *elsewhere*
pancia [páń-ča]	*anche* [áŋ -ke]	*tanto* [tán-to]
mangia [máń-ĵa]	*sangue* [sáŋ-gwe]	*vendo* [vɛ́n-do]
conscio [kóń-ʃo]	*cinque* [číŋ-kwe]	*nome* [nó:-me]

Once again, the palatalization and velarization of /n/ before palatals and velars is an example of assimilation. The complementary distribution of /n/ can now be put into rule form as follows:

$$/n/ \quad \rightarrow \quad \begin{bmatrix} [\acute{n}] \ / \ \_\_ \ C \ [+palatal] \\ [\eta] \ / \ \_\_ \ C \ [+velar] \\ [n] \ / \ elsewhere \end{bmatrix}$$

All double consonants have phonemic status. Commutation tests can, in fact, be set up to show that each one contrasts with: (1) other double consonants, and (2) corresponding single consonants. Here is a sampling of minimal pairs showing these two types of phonemic contrast:

DOUBLE CONSONANT ~ DOUBLE CONSONANT

/p:/ ~ /n:/
ca*pp*a – ca*nn*a

/b:/ ~ /ʃ:/
cono*bb*e – cono*sce*

/t:/ ~ /l:/
fa*tt*o – fa*ll*o

/d:/ ~ /n:/
ca*dd*e – ca*nn*e

/č:/ ~ /n:/
ca*cci*a – ca*nn*a

/ĵ:/ ~ /s:/
le*gg*e – le*ss*e

/k:/ ~ /p:/
ta*cc*o – ta*pp*o

/g:/ ~ /k:/
le*gg*o – le*cc*o

/f:/ ~ /s:/
ba*ff*i – ba*ss*i

/v:/ ~ /l:/
bevve – belle

/s:/ ~ /t:/
rosso – rotto

/ʃ/ ~ /t:/
lascia – latta

/ts:/ ~ /t:/
mezzo – metto

/r:/ ~ /s:/
torre – tosse

/l:/ ~ /t:/
collo ~ cotto

/λ:/ ~ /t:/
figlio ~ fitto

/m:/ ~ /p:/
mamma ~ mappa

/n:/ ~ /t:/
nonni ~ notti

/ń:/ ~ /s:/
bagno ~ basso

DOUBLE CONSONANT ~ CORRESPONDING SINGLE CONSONANT

/t:/ ~ /t/
fatto – fato

/d:/ ~ /d/
cadde – cade

/g:/ ~ /g/
leggo – lego ('I tie')

/v:/ ~ /v/
bevve – beve

/s:/ ~ /s/
ro*ss*a – ro*s*a

/r:/ ~ /r/
ca*rr*o – ca*r*o

/l:/ ~ /l/
be*ll*a ~ be*l*a

/λ:/ ~ /l/
fi*gli*o ~ fi*l*o

/n:/ ~ /n/
no*nn*o ~ no*n*o ('ninth')

/ñ:/ ~ /n/
so*gn*o ~ so*n*o

There are two phonological rules that involve double articulations: syntactic doubling and complementary lengthening. **Syntactic doubling** refers to the process whereby the word boundary between certain function words such as *a, da, sopra,* and so on, which end in a vowel, and a following word beginning with a consonant is eliminated, and the initial consonant of the word doubled. This explanation is an oversimplified characterization of syntactic doubling, which would otherwise require much more substantive treatment than we can give it here. For the present purposes, the rule for syntactic doubling can be formulated as follows (*/...V/ = specific type of word ending in a vowel, # = word boundary, /C.../ = word beginning with a consonant):

*/...V/   #   /C.../ → */...VC:.../

This rule reads as follows:

A specific type of word ending in a vowel (*/...V/), followed respectively by a word boundary (#) and a word beginning with a consonant (/C.../), undergoes a change (→) whereby the boundary is eliminated and the initial consonant of the following word is doubled (*/...VC:.../).

Here are some examples:

da + vero	→	*davvero*	=	[da-v:é:-ro]
sopra + tutto	→	*soprattutto*	=	[so-pra-t:ú-t:o]
a + casa	→	*a(c)casa*	=	[a-k:á:-za]
etc.				

Complementary lengthening is the process whereby a stressed vowel in an open syllable is lengthened, unless it is followed by a double consonant, in which case it is short. The length of the vowel or consonant is said to be a *complementary* feature, because when a vowel and consonant are adjacent in the chain of speech, one or the other can be long, but not both.

STRESSED VOWEL = LONG	STRESSED VOWEL = SHORT
BEFORE A SINGLE CONSONANT	BEFORE A DOUBLE CONSONANT
fato [fá:-to]	*fatto* [fá-t:o]
cade [ká:-de]	*cadde* [ká-d:e]
nono [nɔ́:-no]	*nonno* [nɔ́-n:o]

Complementary lengthening can be shown with the following rule:

> *A stressed vowel in an open syllable is long before a single consonant but short before a double consonant.*

$$\acute{V}\text{-} \quad \rightarrow \quad \begin{bmatrix} \acute{V}\text{:-} & /\underline{\quad} C \\ \acute{V}\text{-} & /\underline{\quad} C\text{:} \end{bmatrix}$$

Distinctive Features

We started off this chapter by characterizing /n/ as a 'prototypical nasal.' This characterization is appropriate, for it indicates that a phoneme is really an abstraction that, in this case, stands for a set of three distinct nasal allophones:

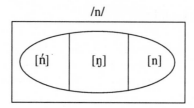

The property [+nasal], known as a **distinctive feature**, is the feature that defines this particular set. In effect, all phonemes are made up of bundles of such features. Take, for instance, the phonemes /p/, /b/, /t/, /d/, /m/, and /n/:

- They all share the feature [+consonantal], since they are all consonants, rather than vowels or glides (semiconsonants and semivowels), which share the feature [+vocalic].
- The phonemes /b/, /d/, /m/, and /n/ are different from /p/ and /t/ by virtue of the fact that they are [+voiced].
- The phonemes /p/, /b/, and /m/ are different from /t/, /d/, and /n/ by virtue of the fact that they are pronounced with the lips and, thus, share the feature [+labial].
- The phonemes /m/ and /n/ share the feature [+nasal], since they are pronounced by expelling the air stream through the nose.

We can now draw up a chart to show which distinctive features are possessed by each phoneme ([+] indicates the presence of a feature, [–] its absence):

	/p/	/t/	/b/	/d/	/m/	/n/
Consonantal	+	+	+	+	+	+
Vocalic	–	–	–	–	–	–
Voiced	–	–	+	+	+	+
Labial	+	–	+	–	+	–
Nasal	–	–	–	–	+	+

This chart makes it possible to pinpoint with precision what differentiates, say, /m/ and /n/ from other consonants: that is, it allows the linguist to identify exactly what feature or features trigger an opposition in a commutation test. Take, for instance, some of the oppositions we have looked at above. The distinctive feature or features that trigger the opposition in each case can now be pinpointed exactly:

/p/ ~ /b/
palla – balla
[–voiced] ~ [+voiced]

/p/ ~ /t/
patto – tatto
[+labial] ~ [–labial]

/p/ ~ /d/
penti – denti
[+labial] ~ [–labial]
[–voiced] ~ [+voiced]

/b/ ~ /m/
banca ~ manca
[–nasal] ~ [+nasal]

/d/ ~ /m/
dare – mare
[–nasal] ~ [+nasal]
[–labial] ~ [+labial]

A distinctive-feature analysis of phonemes makes it possible to write the phonological rules of a language in a more exact way. Take, for instance, the distribution rule for /n/ formulated above. This can now be reformulated as follows:

$$C \; [+nasal] \quad \rightarrow \quad \begin{bmatrix} [+palatal] \; / \; \underline{\quad} \; C \; [+palatal] \\ \\ [+velar] \; / \; \underline{\quad} \; C \; [+velar] \end{bmatrix}$$

This rule shows that a nasal consonant will assimilate to the point of articulation of the following consonant. The features [+palatal] and [+velar], in the case of nasal consonants, are said therefore to be *non-contrastive* because they are *predictable*. When a feature is predictable it is called **redundant**.

Certain features of sounds are, de facto, redundant. For instance, all nasal consonants are [+voiced]. This can be accounted for by a redundancy rule as follows:

If a consonant phoneme is [+nasal], *then it is also* [+voiced].

$$\begin{bmatrix} [\text{+consonantal}] \\ \\ [\text{+nasal}] \end{bmatrix} \rightarrow [\text{+voiced}]$$

Specifying which features are redundant for which phonemes, and which features are unpredictable, constitutes a basic task of a detailed phonological analysis.

Distinctive-Feature Analysis

The distinctive features that are pertinent for a thorough analysis of the Italian vowels, semiconsonants, and semivowels are the following:

	[a]	[e]	[ɛ]	[o]	[ɔ]	[i]	[u]	[y]	[i̯]	[w]	[u̯]
Consonantal	–	–	–	–	–	–	–	+	+	+	+
Vocalic	+	+	+	+	+	+	+	+	+	+	+
High	–	–	–	–	–	+	+	+	+	+	+
Mid	–	+	+	+	+	–	–	–	–	–	–
Low	+	–	–	–	–	–	–	–	–	–	–
Back	–	–	–	+	+	–	+	–	–	+	+
Open	–	–	+	–	+	–	–	–	–	–	–
Close	–	+	–	+	–	–	–	–	–	–	–

Note the following things:

• Any segment marked as [–back] is, of course, also [+front] (which is, of course, a redundancy).
• The glides are distinguished from the vowels by the feature [+consonantal].

We can now conflate the two 'glide-formation' rules described above as follows:

$$
\begin{bmatrix} +\text{vocalic} \\ -\text{consonantal} \\ +\text{high} \end{bmatrix}
\ \rightarrow\ [+\text{consonantal}]
\quad\Big/\quad
\begin{bmatrix} \#\ \underline{\quad}\ [-\text{high}] \\[4pt] [-\text{high}]\ \underline{\quad}\ \# \end{bmatrix}
$$

This rule states the following:

> *Any high vowel (/i/, /u/) becomes a glide ([+consonantal]) before or after a non-high vowel (of the same type) in the same syllable.*

Since this process involves changing one feature [–consonantal] into another one [+consonantal], it is known, logically, as a **feature-changing rule**.

The distinctive features that are relevant for an analysis of the Italian single-consonant phonemes are the following (a *coronal* is a sound articulated by raising the tongue blade towards the hard palate):

	p	b	t	d	č	ĵ	k	g	f	v	s	ʃ	ts	dz	r	l	m	n
Consonantal	+	+	+	+	+	+	+	+	+	+	+	+	+	+	+	+	+	+
Sonorant	−	−	−	−	−	−	−	−	−	−	−	−	−	−	+	+	+	+
Nasal	−	−	−	−	−	−	−	−	−	−	−	−	−	−	−	−	+	+
Voiced	−	+	−	+	−	+	−	+	−	+	−	−	−	+	+	+	+	+
Continuant	−	−	−	−	−	−	−	−	+	+	+	+	−	−	+	+	+	+
Labial	+	+	−	−	−	−	−	−	+	+	−	−	−	−	−	−	+	−
Dental	−	−	+	+	−	−	−	−	−	−	+	−	+	+	−	+	−	+
Palatal	−	−	−	−	+	+	−	−	−	−	−	+	−	−	+	−	−	−
Anterior	+	+	+	+	+	+	−	−	+	+	+	+	+	+	−	−	+	+
Velar	−	−	−	−	−	−	+	+	−	−	−	−	−	−	−	−	−	−
Coronal	−	−	+	+	+	+	−	−	−	−	+	+	+	+	+	+	−	+
Sibilant	−	−	−	−	−	−	−	−	−	−	+	+	−	−	−	−	−	−

Now, the complementary distribution rules for /n/ and /l/ can be conflated into one general rule. Note from the chart that these two phonemes share two features: [+sonorant] and [+coronal]. So, they form a class defined by these two features. The chart also shows that palatals and velars share the feature [−anterior]. Given this information, the rule can now be set out as follows:

$$\begin{bmatrix} +\text{consonantal} \\ +\text{sonorant} \\ +\text{coronal} \end{bmatrix} \rightarrow [-\text{anterior}] \ / \ \underline{\quad} \ \begin{bmatrix} +\text{consonantal} \\ -\text{anterior} \end{bmatrix}$$

The specification to the left of the arrow indicates those features that distinguish /n/ and /l/ from other phonemes. So, again, this rule makes it explicit that the feature [–anterior] is predictable in the case of the /n/ and /l/. The assimilation process in this case can be characterized as one in which the [-anterior] feature is 'added on' to the nasals and laterals. This is known, logically, as an **addition rule**.

A distinctive-feature analysis of /s/ shows the [+voiced] feature is predictable:

$$\begin{bmatrix} +\text{consonantal} \\ +\text{sibilant} \\ +\text{dental} \end{bmatrix} \rightarrow [+\text{voiced}] \ / \ \underline{\quad} \ \begin{bmatrix} +\text{consonantal} \\ +\text{voiced} \end{bmatrix}$$
$$[+\text{vocalic}] \ \underline{\quad} \ [+\text{vocalic}]$$

This rule states the following:

> *A dental sibilant will become voiced either in front of a voiced consonant or between vowels.*

The double consonants can now be shown to be distinguishable from the single consonants in terms of the feature [+length]. So, the process of syntactic doubling can now be reformulated as follows (ø = deletion, [+syllabic] = nuclear vowel, [+stress] = primary stress):

$$*\ldots[+\text{vocalic}] \quad \# \begin{bmatrix} +\text{consonantal} \\ -\text{length} \end{bmatrix} \rightarrow *\ldots[+\text{vocalic}] \quad \text{ø} \begin{bmatrix} +\text{consonantal} \\ +\text{length} \end{bmatrix}$$

The rule shows that, given the presence of certain forms ending in a vowel, the word boundary (#) is deleted (ø) and the [–length] feature of the following consonant is changed to [+length]. This is really a two-tiered rule: (1) it shows the change of [–length] to [+length], which is, of course, a *feature-changing* process, and (2) it shows the deletion of the word boundary, which is a **deletion** process.

Follow-Up Activities

1. In your own words, elaborate on the idea that knowledge of how to use the sounds of Italian to pronounce words goes beyond the ability to produce all the phonically different sounds of Italian.

2. In your own words, explain the difference between phonetic description and phonological analysis.

3. What three tasks are involved in the analysis of sound systems?

4. Define the following terms:

   phoneme
   minimal pair
   commutation test
   contrast
   free variation
   allophone
   complementary distribution
   phonological rule
   assimilation
   syntactic doubling
   complementary lengthening
   distinctive feature
   redundant feature
   feature-changing rule
   addition rule
   deletion rule

5. What vocalic phonemic contrast does each of the following minimal pairs reveal?

   Example: costa – casta = /o/ ~ /a/

santo – sento
pongo – pungo
corta – carta
maglie – moglie
contare – cantare
inno – anno
urto – arto
pasta – pista
pista – posta
corretto – corrotto
vino – vano

6. For each of the following contrasts, provide three minimal pairs to show phonemic status:

   Example: /a/ ~ /u/

           basta – busta, cara – cura, capo – cupo

   /a/ ~ /i/
   /a/ ~ /u/
   /a/ ~ /e/
   /a/ ~ /o/
   /i/ ~ /u/
   /i/ ~ /e/
   /i/ ~ /o/
   /u/ ~ /e/
   /u/ ~ /o/
   /e/ ~ /o/

7. Give the complementary distribution rule pertaining to semiconsonants and semivowels.

8. What consonantal phonemic contrast does each minimal pair reveal?

   Example: patto – fatto = /p/ ~ /f/
              fato – fatto = /t/ ~ /t:/

   pane – cane
   toro – foro

osso – otto
canto – tanto
cento – vento
faccia – fascia
gente – mente
pungono – purgono
palco – parco
rosa – roba
rosa – rossa
coglie – colle
sogno – sonno

9. For each of the following contrasts, provide three minimal pairs to show phonemic status:

Example: /p/ ~ /b/
          pasta – basta, palla – balla, pelle – belle

/p/ ~ /p:/
/t/ ~ /d/
/t/ ~ /d:/
/t:/ ~ /d:/
/č/ ~ /ĵ/
/č/ ~ /č:/
/ĵ:/ ~ /k:/
/k/ ~ /g/
/k/ ~ /k:/
/g:/ ~ /n:/
/f/ ~ /v/
/s/ ~ /ʃ/
/s:/ ~ /s/
/s:/ ~ /ʃ:/
/r/ ~ /l/
/r/ ~ /r:/
/l/ ~ /l:/
/m/ ~ /n/
/λ:/ ~ /l/
/ń:/ ~ /n:/
/λ:/ ~ /l:/
/ń:/ ~ /n:/

10. Give the complementary distribution rules for /s/, /l/, and /n/.

11. Give the appropriate phonological rules for syntactic doubling and complementary lengthening.

12. Why is distinctive-feature analysis a highly precise tool for conducting the phonological analysis of a language?

13. Review your answers to questions 5 and 8 above. Now, give the distinctive feature(s) that trigger(s) the contrast in each case.

> *Example:*   costa – casta
> /o/ ~ /a/
> [+mid] ~ [–mid]
> [–low] ~ [+low]
> [+back] ~ [–back]

santo – sento
pongo – pungo
corta – carta
maglie – moglie
contare – cantare
inno – anno
urto – arto
pasta – pista
pista – posta
corretto – corrotto
vino – vano
pane – cane
toro – foro
osso – otto
canto – tanto
cento – vento
faccia – fascia
gente – mente
palco – parco
rosa – roba
rosa – rossa
coglie – colle
sogno – sonno

14. Give examples of feature-changing rules in Italian.

15. Give an example of a deletion rule in Italian.

5
Word Structure

··

A good word is as a good tree – its roots are firm, and its branches are in heaven; it gives its produce every season by the leave of its Lord.

Qur'an

In the previous two chapters we have been describing the pronunciation of words, without having defined what a *word* is. As we have seen, a word is, essentially, a form made up of speech sounds serving to communicate meaning. A word that conveys a 'single piece of meaning' is known more technically as a *minimal free form*. But not all words are free forms. For instance, the word *illogical* is 'segmentable' into smaller units that also have meaning: (1) the basic free form, *logic*, which has a 'dictionary meaning,' (2) the negative prefix *il-*, which has a recurring functional meaning ('opposite of'), and (3) the suffix *-al*, which also has a functional meaning ('the act or process of being something').

The study of how words are formed in a language and what 'bits of pieces' can coalesce into the make-up and meaning of words comes under the rubric of **morphology**. These may be: roots (as the *rasp-*, in *raspberry*), free forms (*logic, play, boy*), endings (as the *-s* in *boys, -ed* in *played,* and *-ing* in *playing*), prefixes and suffixes (as the *il-* and *-al* in *illogical*), or internal alterations indicating such grammatical categories as tense (*sing – sang*), and number (*mouse – mice*).

Words

Words can be distinguished in terms of: (1) their dictionary meaning, in which case they are called *lexical items*; (2) the various phonic forms they manifest in the language, known as *syntactic forms*; or (3) how their forms are pronounced, known as *phonological forms*. Consider the form *learn*. First, note that it has a dictionary meaning, designating 'to gain knowledge or skill.' Second, note that forms such as *learned* and *learning* are not lexically distinct words. Rather, they are different *syntactic forms* of the same lexical item. Third, note that the form *learned* can have two pronunciations: (1) when it is the verbal past tense it is pronounced as one syllable; (2) when it is used as an adjective (as in 'the *learned* professor'), it is pronounced with two syllables.

Words come naturally to the human species. When a child reaches six months, she starts to emit monosyllabic forms (*mu, ma, da, di*, etc.), which are imitations of words she has heard in meaningful situations. These are called **holophrastic** (one-word) utterances, because they are, in effect, expressions that have been shown to serve three basic functions: (1) naming an object and event; (2) expressing an action or a desire for some action; and (3) conveying emotional states. Holophrases are phonic reductions of adult lexical items – *da* for *dog*, *ca* for *cat*, and so forth. Over 60 per cent will develop into nouns, and 20 per cent will become verbs during the second year, when children typically start doubling their holophrases — *wowo* 'water,' *bubu* 'bottle, *mama* 'mother,' and so on.

The Morpheme

The basic unit of word-formation is called the **morpheme**. The word *cats,* for instance, consists of two morphemes: *cat,* whose meaning can be roughly rendered as 'feline animal,' and *-s*, whose meaning is 'more than one.' *Antimicrobial,* meaning 'capable of destroying microorganisms,' can be divided into three morphemes: *anti-* ('against'), *microbe* ('microorganism'), and *-ial* (a suffix that makes the word an adjective).

A morpheme can be defined as the smallest unit of sound that bears a meaning. If the meaning is lexical (dictionary), then it is called a *lexical morpheme*, or **lexeme**; if it is purely grammatical (e.g., the *-s* in *cats*), it is called a **grammatical morpheme**. The Italian word *incautamente*, for instance, is made up of three morphemes:

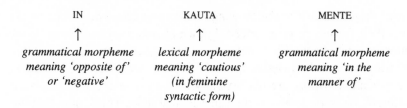

The process of identifying morphemes is known as **segmentation**, since it entails segmenting a word into forms that cannot be split any further. The forms /in-/, /kauto/, and /-mente/ cannot, in fact, be segmented any further. Note that morphemes are represented by phonemic notation. This is why the semivowel in /kauto/ is represented as /u/, rather than as the allophone [ṷ], and why the nasal in /-mente/ is represented as /n/, rather than allophonically as [ŋ]. For the sake of convenience, syllable structure is also generally not indicated in morphemic representation:

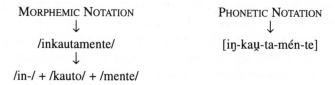

The essential criterion in segmentation is that a morpheme is established when a sound or sequence of sounds cannot be divided further into meaning-bearing segments. Linguists identify morphemic segments by comparing words in a systematic manner. Take, for instance, the following forms found in Swahili, a northern Bantu (African) language:

1. *nitasoma*   'I will read'
2. *nilisoma*   'I read (past)'
3. *utasoma*   'you will read'
4. *ulisoma*   'you read (past)'

By comparing these forms systematically, it is possible to establish the following facts:

• Since /-soma/ occurs in all four forms, it can be deduced that it is a lexical morpheme which has a meaning that corresponds to English 'read.'

- Comparing the first two forms against the last two, we can see that the morpheme /ni-/ corresponds to the English pronoun 'I' and /u-/ to the pronoun 'you.'
- Comparing the first and second forms in tandem with the third and fourth, we can deduce that /-ta-/ is a future-tense grammatical morpheme and /-li-/ a past-tense grammatical morpheme.

Morphemes are of two kinds: *free* and *bound*. In the word *incauta-mente*, only the middle morpheme /kauto/ can occur by itself as an autonomous word, *cauto*. It is thus a **free morpheme**. On the other hand, /in-/ and /-mente/ must be attached to other morphemes. They are thus known as **bound morphemes.**

There are two subtypes of bound morphemes. Recall the form *learned* mentioned above. This consists of the free lexical morpheme /learn/ plus the bound grammatical morpheme /-ed/. The /-ed/ in this case is known as an **inflectional morpheme** because it provides further information about /learn/, namely that the action of learning has occurred in the past. On the other hand, the grammatical morpheme /-mente/, as in *cautamente*, has a different function: it serves to create a word with a different grammatical function than the word to which it is bound — the word *cauto* is an adjective, while *cautamente* is an adverb. This kind of morpheme is called **derivational.**

We can now see that the organization of the three morphemic segments in *incautamente* has a hierarchical arrangement: that is, this form is constructed by taking the adjective stem /kauto/, adding the derivational morpheme /-mente/ to it, which serves to change its syntactic class from adjective to adverb, and prefixing /in-/ to the 'embedded' adjectival stem. Its hierarchical structure can be shown with a tree diagram as follows:

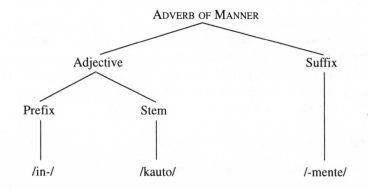

A type of bound morpheme that requires special mention, given its frequency in the formation of words in languages across the world, is the **affix**. This is defined as a bound morpheme that is attached to other morphemes in specific positions. The /in-/ and /-mente/ in *incautamente* are examples of affixes. The former is known more specifically as a **prefix** because it is attached before another morpheme; the latter is known as a **suffix** because it is attached after another morpheme. There are two other types of affixes that linguists discuss: *infixes* and *circumfixes*. An **infix** is an affix that is inserted into another morpheme. For example, observe the following words in Bantoc, a language spoken in the Philippines:

1. *fikas*   'strong'   →   *fumikas*   'to be strong'
2. *kilad*   'red'   →   *kumilad*   'to be red'
3. *fusul*   'enemy'   →   *fumusul*   'to be an enemy'

As can be seen, inserting /-um-/ after the initial consonant adds the meaning 'to be' to the lexical morpheme. A similar infixation process occurs in the case of some third-conjugation verbs in Italian:

THIRD CONJUGATION WITHOUT INFIXATION	THIRD CONJUGATION WITH INFIXATION
parto 'I leave' /part-/ + /-o/	*capisco* 'I understand' /kap-/ + /-isk-/ + /-o/
dormo 'I sleep' /dorm-/ + /-o/	*finisco* 'I finish' /fin-/ + /-isk-/ + /-o/
apro 'I open' /apr-/ + /-o/	*preferisco* 'I prefer' /prefer-/ + /-isk-/ + /-o/

In such words, the /part-/ and /kap-/ segments are known as **root** or **stem morphemes**. **Circumfixes** are affixes that come 'as a package,' so to speak, since they are attached to a root morpheme both initially and finally. For example, in Chickasaw, a Native language spoken in Oklahoma, negation is rendered by attaching both the prefix /ik-/ and the suffix /-o/ to a root (in place of the final vowel):

lakna 'it is yellow'   →   *iklakno* 'it isn't yellow'

palli 'it is hot'   →   *ikpallo* 'it isn't hot'

Allomorphs

The actual pronunciation that a morpheme takes will depend on several factors. Take the inflectional plural morpheme /-s/ in English. In actual fact, this morpheme has more than one phonic realization, as can be seen in the following chart. (Note that the vowel in /-əs/ represents a low mid vowel known as *schwa*):

1. /-s/	2. /-əz/	3. /-əs/
lot + /-s/ → lots	load + /-z/ → loads	lass + /-es/ → lasses
top + /-s/ → tops	dog + /-z/ → dogs	church + /-es/ → churches
kick + /-s/ → kicks	bra + /-z/ → bras	judge + /-es/ → judges

Column (1) contains root forms that end in any voiceless consonant except a sibilant or affricate; column (2) contains root forms that end in a voiced segment, either a voiced consonant (except a sibilant or affricate) or a vowel; and column (3) contains root forms that end in any sibilant or affricate. This suggests, of course, a rule of complementary distribution:

> *The plural morpheme in English is realized as /-s/ when it is attached to a form ending in a voiceless consonant (except a sibilant or affricate), as /-z/ when it is attached to a form ending in a voiced consonant (except a sibilant or affricate) or vowel, or else as /-əs/ when it is attached to a form ending in a sibilant or affricate.*

The predictable realizations /-s/, /-z/, and /-əs/ are known as **allomorphs**. In the above case, the allomorphs are *phonologically conditioned* variants because they vary according to the final phoneme of the morpheme to which they are attached. The complementary distribution of such allomorphs is called *morphophonemic*.

The indefinite article presents another case of morphophonemic variation in English:

1. /a/
   a boy
   a girl
   a friend
   a mother
   a father

2. /æn/
an egg
an island
an apple
an opera

As can be easily seen from a comparison of the forms in (1) and (2), the allomorph /a/ occurs before a morpheme beginning with consonant and /æn/ before a morpheme beginning with a vowel. There are two ways in which to show this formally (/Indef/ = indefinite article morpheme):

1.   /Indef/   →

$$\begin{bmatrix} /a/ \ / \_ \ \#C \ldots \# \\ /æn/ \ / \_ \ \#V \ldots \# \end{bmatrix}$$

2.   /a/   →   /æn/ / __ #V ... #

Rule (1) does not assume that one or the other of the allomorphs is the 'default' variant for the indefinite article morpheme. Rule (2) assumes that /a/ is the basic form and that /æn/ is the conditioned variant. Either type of rule will 'do the job' equally well, so to speak. More specifically, the conditioned variant is called the **marked** form, whereas the unconditioned, or default one, is called the **unmarked** form. The latter is the form that is most typical, or representative (nonspecific), of a class. In Italian, the masculine plural form, as for instance in *i turisti*, is unmarked, because it can refer (nonspecifically) to any tourist, male or female, whereas the feminine plural form, *le turiste*, is marked, since it refers specifically to female tourists.

The Italian indefinite article also undergoes morphophonemic variation, but, in addition, its variation is affected by grammatical factors:

1. /uno/

uno zio	'an uncle'
uno zero	'a zero'
uno studente	'a student'
uno sbaglio	'a mistake'

2. /un/

un ragazzo	'a boy'
un padre	'a father'
un figlio	'a son'
un tetto	'a roof'
un amico	'a friend (male)'
un uomo	'a man'
un occhio	'an eye'
un impiego	'a job'

3. /una/

una zia	'an aunt'
una ragazza	'a girl'
una smania	'a fit'
una figlia	'a daughter'

4. /un/

un'opera	'an opera'
un'amica	'a friend (female)'
un'isola	'an island'
un'epoca	'an epoch'

The first thing to note is that the allomorphic choice is determined, in part, by the gender of the following noun: [+m] = masculine, [+f] = feminine. Second, the choice is further constrained by the initial sound of the noun. Limiting our observations only to the above set of data, we can see that: (1) if the masculine noun begins with /ts/, /dz/, /sC/ (C = consonant), then the allomorph is /uno/, otherwise it is /un/; (2) if the feminine noun begins with any consonant, then the allomorph used is /una/, but if it begins with a vowel, then it is /un/. The following distribution rule summarizes these observations ([+noun] = noun, C = any consonant, C_1 = /ts/, /dz/, /ñ/, C_2 = C – C_1 [i.e., any consonant other than C1], V = any vowel):

$$/\text{Indef}/ \quad \rightarrow \quad \begin{bmatrix} /\text{uno}/ & / \_\_ \ \#C1 \dots [+\text{noun}, +\text{m}]\# \\ /\text{un}/ & / \_\_ \ \#C2 \dots [+\text{noun}, +\text{m}]\# \\ /\text{un}/ & / \_\_\#V \dots [+\text{noun}, +\text{m}] \\ /\text{una}/ & / \_\_ \ \#C \dots [+\text{noun}, +\text{f}]\# \\ /\text{un}/ & / \_\_ \ \#V \dots [+\text{noun}, +\text{f}]\# \end{bmatrix}$$

Morphological Analysis

Whereas we could easily elaborate a fairly complete phonological analysis of the Italian sound system in the previous chapter, it would be a much lengthier and more complex task to describe the complete morphological system of Italian here. So, our discussion will be highly selective, focusing on two morphological topics: (1) the definite article and (2) noun gender

The definite article morpheme of Italian can be represented as /Def/. The first thing to note is that it is a *free grammatical morpheme* that occurs mainly before a noun or adjective. Now, consider its allomorphic realizations, which are charted below:

MASCULINE		FEMININE	
1(a)		1(b)	
lo zio	*the uncle*	*la* zia	*the aunt*
gli zii	*the uncles*	*le* zie	*the aunts*
lo zero	*the zero*	*la* zuppa	*the soup*
gli zeri	*the zeroes*	*le* zuppe	*the soups*
2(a)		2(b)	
lo studente	*the student*	*la* studentessa	*the student*
gli studenti	*the students*	*le* studentesse	*the students*
lo sbaglio	*the mistake*	*la* smania	*the fit*
gli sbagli	*the mistakes*	*le* smanie	*the fits*
3(a)		3(b)	
il regalo	*the gift*	*la* madre	*the mother*
i regali	*the gifts*	*le* madri	*the mothers*
il marito	*the husband*	*la* delizia	*the delight*
i mariti	*the husbands*	*le* delizie	*the delights*
4(a)		4(b)	
*l'*occhio	*the eye*	*l'*aria	*the air*
gli occhi	*the eyes*	*le* arie	*the airs*
*l'*impero	*the empire*	*l'*ora	*the hour*
gli imperi	*the empires*	*le* ore	*the hours*

Comparing the forms in all the (a) sections of the chart with those in the (b) sections shows that the gender of the noun is a factor in constraining the selection of the allomorph, although it is not the only factor. Thus, in our distribution analysis, we can take this into account by using the notation [+m] = *masculine*, [+f] = *feminine*. We also note that the grammatical number of the noun has an influence on the allomorphic choice. We can take this fact into account by using the notation [+s] = *singular*, [–s] = *plural*.

Now we note that morphophonemic factors condition the distribution:

- By contrasting 1(a) and 2(a) against 3(a), we can see that the initial consonant of the masculine noun influences the allomorphic choice: before /ts/, /dz/, and /sC/ (where C = consonant), the allomorph used is /lo/ if the noun ([+noun]) is singular and /λi/ if it is plural; before a masculine noun beginning with any other consonant, the allomorph used is /il/ if the noun is singular and /i/ if it is plural. To complete the description, it should be mentioned that these allomorphs are also used before masculine nouns beginning with /ń/ (*lo gnocco, gli gnocchi*), /y/ (*lo iugoslavo, gli iugoslavi*), and /ps/ (*lo psicologo, gli psicologi*).

- By comparing 1(a), 2(a), and 3(a) with 1(b), 2(b), and 3(b), we can see that the same type of distribution does not apply to feminine nouns. In this case, the distribution is as follows: before a feminine noun beginning with any consonant the allomorph used is /la/ if the noun is singular and /le/ if it is plural.

- By comparing 4(a) and 4(b) with the others, we can see that if the noun starts with a vowel (V), then one allomorph /l/ (written *l'*) is used before both masculine and feminine singular nouns. In the plural, the allomorph /λi/ is used before masculine nouns and the allomorph /le/ before feminine nouns.

The above observations can be synthesized into a distribution rule as follows. Note that the same distribution applies when /Def/ occurs before an adjective or other kind of nominal (e.g., a verb that has been nominalized, such as *il mangiare*). We will use the following symbols: [+noun] = noun, V = vowel, C = any consonant, S_1 = /y/, C_1 = /ts, dz, ń/, C_2 = $C - C_1$ (i.e., any consonant other than C_1).

$$/\text{Def}/ \rightarrow \begin{bmatrix}
/\text{lo}/ \ / \ \_\_ & \#S_1 \ldots [+\text{noun}, +\text{m}, +\text{s}]\# \\
/\text{lo}/ \ / \ \_\_ & \#C_1 \ldots [+\text{noun}, +\text{m}, +\text{s}]\# \\
/\text{lo}/ \ / \ \_\_ & \#/\text{ps}/ \ldots [+\text{noun}, +\text{m}, +\text{s}]\# \\
/\text{il}/ \ / \ \_\_ & \#C_2 \ldots [+\text{noun}, +\text{m}, +\text{s}]\# \\
/\text{la}/ \ / \ \_\_ & \#C \ldots [+\text{noun}, +\text{f}, +\text{s}]\# \\
/\text{l}/ \ / \ \_\_ & \#V \ldots [+\text{noun}, +\text{m}, +\text{s}]\# \\
/\text{l}/ \ / \ \_\_ & \#V \ldots [+\text{noun}, +\text{f}, +\text{s}]\# \\
/\lambda\text{i}/ \ / \ \_\_ & \#V \ldots [+\text{noun}, +\text{m}, -\text{s}]\# \\
/\lambda\text{i}/ \ / \ \_\_ & \#S_1 \ldots [+\text{noun}, +\text{m}, -\text{s}]\# \\
/\lambda\text{i}/ \ / \ \_\_ & \#C_1 \ldots [+\text{noun}, +\text{m}, -\text{s}]\# \\
/\lambda\text{i}/ \ / \ \_\_ & \#/\text{ps}/ \ldots [+\text{noun}, +\text{m}, -\text{s}]\# \\
/\text{i}/ \ / \ \_\_ & \#C_2 \ldots [+\text{noun}, +\text{m}, -\text{s}]\# \\
/\text{le}/ \ / \ \_\_ & \#C \ldots [+\text{noun}, +\text{f}, -\text{s}]\# \\
/\text{le}/ \ / \ \_\_ & \#V \ldots [+\text{noun}, +\text{f}, -\text{s}]\#
\end{bmatrix}$$

This rule is read as follows:

/Def/ is realized as: (from top to bottom) /lo/ before a masculine singular noun beginning with S_1 = /y/, C_1 = /ts, dz, ń/, or /ps/; /il/ before a masculine singular noun beginning with C_2 = any other consonant; /la/ before a feminine singular noun beginning with any consonant; /l/ before a singular noun, masculine or feminine, beginning with any vowel; /λi/ before a masculine singular noun beginning with any vowel, S_1 = /y/, C_1 = /ts, dz, ń/, or /ps/; /le/ before any feminine plural noun beginning with any consonant or vowel.

A similar type of distributional rule can be devised for the allomorphs of the demonstrative *quello* and the adjective *bello* (when it occurs before the noun).

In describing gender assignment, it is necessary to note, first, that the masculine gender is typically the unmarked one. This can be seen in the plural forms of nouns as follows:

MASCULINE PLURAL FORMS
i turisti = *all tourists, males and females*
gli amici = *all friends, males and females*

FEMININE PLURAL FORMS
le turiste = *female tourists*
le amiche = *female friends*

Recall from above that an unmarked form is the one considered to represent the entire category to which it belongs. The gender system of a language is said to be *natural* insofar as it requires that male human beings be named with the masculine gender and that female human beings be named with the feminine gender. In this way the morphemic units used allow speakers to refer to the biological sex of human referents. Nouns of this type have also been called *referential* and *isomorphic*. For inanimate referents, the conventional view is that gender assignment is unpredictable and therefore arbitrary. Nouns of this type are said to show *grammatical gender* only; this is *nonreferential* and *nonisomorphic*. For example, there appears to be no natural link between the grammatical gender of a word like *casa* (which is feminine) and its referent ('house'). This view has been somewhat modified by recent research, which brings forward evidence to suggest that the gender of nouns referring to inanimate referents tends, through metaphorical extension, to be assigned to the category perceived to indicate some biological property of the referents.

Let us look more closely at the so-called *natural gender system*. This is a symmetrical one: nouns that end in the bound morpheme /-o/ are masculine and normally refer to male beings (*ragazzo* = 'boy'), whereas those that end in /-a/ are feminine and normally refer to female beings (*ragazza* = 'girl'). There are few exceptions to this rule: only a handful of nouns ending in /-o/ refer to female beings (*il soprano* = 'the soprano'), and only a few ending in /-a/ refer to male beings (*il poeta* = 'poet'). In addition, some nouns ending in /-e/ can be either masculine or feminine: *padre* = 'father' (masculine), *madre* = 'mother' (feminine). Note that this contrast is maintained in other ways — for example, with different suffix morphemes (*elefante* 'male elephant' vs. *elefantessa* 'female elephant'), with different final vowel alternations (*infermiere* 'male nurse' vs. *infermiera* 'female nurse'), and with other kinds of structural devices. However, the /-o/ vs. /-a/ opposition appears to be the most productive one.

In the case of the natural system, the masculine gender is considered to be the unmarked one:

UNMARKED	MARKED
amico	amica
male friend and *friend in general*	*female friend*
tedesco	tedesca
male German and *German in general*	*female German*
gatto	gatta
male cat and *cat in general*	*female cat*

This applies to the plural forms as well: *amici* ('friends in general'), *tedeschi* ('Germans in general'), *gatti* ('cats in general'), and so forth. The rule of gender assignment in the case of the natural gender system is as follows (N [+hum] = noun referring to a human referent):

$$
N\ [+hum]\ \rightarrow\ \left[
\begin{array}{l}
\textit{/\# ... o/} \\
\qquad\qquad\Big/\quad [+male]\ /\ [-sex] \\
\textit{/\# ... e/} \\
\ \\
\textit{/\# ... a/} \\
\qquad\qquad\Big/\quad [+female]\ /\ [+sex] \\
\textit{/\# ... e/}
\end{array}
\right]
$$

This rule is read as follows:

> *A noun referring to a human referent is assigned an /-o/ or /-e/ ending if the referent is male or unmarked for sex ([-sex]); it is assigned an /-a/ or /-e/ ending if the referent is female or marked for sex ([+sex]).*

The rule is, needless to say, incomplete, since it does not take into account nouns such as *elefante* and *elefantessa*. These alternations would have to be incorporated into a larger, more comprehensive rule.

We conclude the discussion of gender assignment on a sociological note. Recent studies suggest that grammatical categories are not impervious to social attitudes and perceptions. The propensity to evaluate various aspects of reality in terms of grammatical categories exposes language as a psychologically powerful modelling instrument, ready to serve our variable and ever-changing perceptions of the world. Even a firm grammatical relation like markedness will collapse under the weight of social change. The use of the masculine as the unmarked gender category and the feminine as the marked one in Italian might indeed entail negative perceptions of females as inferior to males. Fortunately, Italian, like any language, is ductile enough for its speakers to make personal and social adjustments to meet their changing attitudes and perceptions. Indeed, once we realize that we can construct any word we please without incurring any sexual stereotypes, then we can avoid encoding psychological and social imbalances grammatically. This is why, today, marked words like *avvocatessa* are finally being eliminated from the grammar of Italian.

Affixation

Recall from above that there are four types of affixes: prefixes, suffixes, infixes, and circumfixes. We will illustrate affixation in Italian by looking at one example of each type, except circumfixes, since there are none in Italian.

Let us start with prefixation. Recall the word *incautamente* used several times above. The prefix /in-/ in this case has the meaning 'opposite of, negative.' Now, consider the following words which also have this prefix or its variants:

1.

logico	→	illogico	*illogical*
lecito	→	illecito	*illicit*
leso	→	illeso	*unhurt*

2.

probabile	→	improbabile	*improbable*
possibile	→	impossibile	*impossible*
bocca	→	imboccare	*to spoon-feed*

3.

regolare	→	irregolare	*irregular*
rilevante	→	irrilevante	*irrelevant*
responsabile	→	irresponsabile	*irresponsible*

4.

grosso	→	ingrosso	*wholesale*
saputa	→	insaputa	*unknown*
tollerabile	→	intollerabile	*intolerable*

The above examples show that /in-/ is, predictably, sensitive to phonic environment. The forms in (1) show that the /n/ in the prefix /in-/ assimilates totally to the following [l]; those in (2) that it assimilates partially to the following [p] and [b]; those in (3) that it assimilates totally to the following [r]; and those in (4) that it remains as /n/ in front of all other consonants, with predictable allophonic variation (i.e., *ingrosso* = /in-/ + /grosso/ = [iŋ-gró-s:o]). It can thus be concluded that the prefix /in-/ has four allomorphs, /in-/, /il-/, /ir-/, and /im-/, which are conditioned by the initial consonant of the morpheme to which it is attached: (1) /il-/ before a morpheme that begins with /l/; (2) /ir-/ before one that begins with /r/; (3) /im-/ before one that begins with /p/ or /b/; and (4) /in-/ before a morpheme beginning with any other type of sound:

$$
/\text{in-}/ \quad \rightarrow \quad
\begin{bmatrix}
/\text{il-}/ \,/\, \underline{\quad} \,/\text{l}/ \,\ldots\, \# \\
/\text{ir-}/ \,/\, \underline{\quad} \,/\text{r}/ \,\ldots\, \# \\
/\text{im-}/ \,/\, \underline{\quad} \,/\text{p}/ \,\ldots\, \# \\
/\text{im-}/ \,/\, \underline{\quad} \,/\text{b}/ \,\ldots\, \# \\
/\text{in-}/ \,/\, \text{elsewhere}
\end{bmatrix}
$$

As a case of suffixation, consider the suffix /-is:imo/ ('very'):

1.

bello	→	bellissimo	*very beautiful*
alto	→	altissimo	*very tall*
forte	→	fortissimo	*very strong*
grande	→	grandissimo	*very big*
veloce	→	velocissimo	*very fast*

2.

simpatico	→	simpaticissimo	*very nice*
pratico	→	praticissimo	*very practical*
classico	→	classicissimo	*very classical*

3.

poco	→	pochissimo	*very little*
stanco	→	stanchissimo	*very tired*
lungo	→	lunghissimo	*very long*

4.

| celebre | → | celeberrimo | *very famous* |
| acre | → | acerrimo | *very bitter* |

Ignoring the phonemic differences between the forms in (2) and (3) for now, from a comparison of the forms in (1), (2), and (3), we can see that the suffixation of /-is:imo/ entails the deletion of the previous vowel:

/bello/ + /-is:imo/ → /bell ø/ + /-is:imo/ → /bellis:imo/
/grande/ + /-i:simo/ → /grand ø/ + /-is:imo/ → /grandis:imo
/poko/ + /-is:imo/ → /pok ø/ + /is:imo/ → /pokis:imo/

In general:

/#...o/ + /-is:imo/ → /#...ø/ + /-is:imo/ → /#...is:imo/

Now, the forms in (4) reveal that if the adjective ends in /# ... Cre/ (C = consonant), then the allomorphic variant /-er:imo/ is attached instead and the /r/ and /e/ are deleted:

/čelebre/ + /-is:imo/ → /čeleb ø ø/ + /-er:imo/ → /čeleber:imo/
/akre/ + /-is:imo/ → /ač ø ø/ + /-er:imo/ → /ačer:imo/

In general:

/#...re/ + /-is:imo/ → /#...ø ø/ + /-er:imo/ → /#...er:imo/

The forms in (2) and (3) reveal, moreover, that if the adjective ends in /-ko/ or /-go/, then the velar plosive is palatalized if palatalization is a characteristic of the pluralization of the adjective:

SINGULAR →	PLURAL →	SUFFIXATION		
/simpatico/ →	/simpatiči/	+ /-is:imo/ →	/simpatič ø/ + /-is:imo/ →	/simpatič is:imo/

In general:

| /#...ko/ → | /#...či/ + | /-is:imo/ → | /#...č ø/ + /-is:imo/ → | /#...čis:imo/ |

An interesting case of infixation can be found in the conjugation of verbs like *capire, scolpire,* and *finire.* Morphologically, there are two types of third-conjugation verbs in Italian. Type (1) verbs are conjugated without the infixation. Observe, for instance, the present indicative forms of *scoprire*:

	SCOPRIRE → SCOPR-	
(io)	scopro	*I leave, I am leaving*
(tu)	scopri	*you leave, you are leaving*
(Lei)	scopre	*you leave, you are leaving*
(lui / lei)	scopre	*he / she leaves, he / she is leaving*
(noi)	scopriamo	*we leave, we are leaving*
(voi)	scoprite	*you leave, you are leaving*
(loro)	scoprono	*they leave, they are leaving*

Type (2) verbs are conjugated with the addition of the infix /-isk-/ to the conjugation pattern.

SCOLPIRE → SCOLP-

(io)	scolp*isc*o	*I sculpt, I am sculpting*
(tu)	scolp*isc*i	*you sculpt, you are sculpting*
(Lei)	scolp*isc*e	*you sculpt, you are sculpting*
(lui / lei)	scolp*isc*e	*he/she sculpts, he/she is sculpting*
(noi)	scolp*iamo*	*we sculpt, we are sculpting*
(voi)	scolp*ite*	*you sculpt, you are sculpting*
(loro)	scolp*isc*ono	*they sculpt, they are sculpting*

There are two things to note. First, the /-isk-/ infix is not attached to the first- and second-person plural forms. This entails, of course, a deletion rule Second, the /k/ in /-isk-/ is palatalized before the suffixes /-i/ and /-e/, which are both [-back] vowels.

Follow-Up Activities

1. What are some popular misconceptions about what a *word* is?

2. Define the following notions in your own words.

morphology
holophrase
morpheme
lexeme
grammatical morpheme
segmentation
free morpheme
bound morpheme
inflectional morpheme
derivational morpheme
affix
prefix
suffix
infix
root or stem morpheme
circumfix

allomorph
marked category or form
unmarked category or form

3. Using the segmentation technique, identify fully the morphemes
   in the following words. Use phonemic transcription only.

Example: prefigurazione
        /pre-/   =   bound grammatical morpheme (prefix)
        /figura/   =   free lexical morpheme (lexeme, root)
        /-tsione/ =   bound grammatical morpheme (suffix)

amicizia
prevedibile
incomprensibile
veramente
insincero
improbabile
sopravvivenza
summenzionato
verosimile
velocità
velocissimo
disfunzionalità
incongruo
capostazione
portalettere
attaccabrighe
verosimilitudine

4. By the method of comparison, determine the relevant morphemic
   facts that can be gleaned from each set of forms.

Example: parlo   *I speak*   parli   *you speak*
        scrivo   *I write*   scrivi   *you write*
        etc.
Morphemic Analysis: The bound morpheme /-o/ added to a verbal
root morpheme renders the first-person singular subject pronoun

I; the bound morpheme /-i/, on the other hand, renders the second-person singular subject pronoun *you*.

a.

il mio nome	*my name*	i miei nomi	*my names*
il tuo sospiro	*your sigh*	i tuoi sospiri	*your sighs*
la mia piuma	*my feather*	le mie piume	*my feathers*
la tua aria	*your air*	le tue arie	*your airs*

b.

impero	*realm*	bellezza	*beauty*
dono	*gift*	vita	*life*
fato	*fate*	costanza	*constancy*
marito	*husband*	smania	*fit*
cuore	*heart*	madre	*mother*
furore	*furor*	amante	*lover*

c.

impero	*empire*	imperi	*empires*
dono	*gift*	doni	*gifts*
marito	*husband*	mariti	*husbands*
occhio	*eye*	occhi	*eyes*
zio	*uncle*	zii	*uncles*
sbaglio	*mistake*	sbagli	*mistakes*
pensiero	*thought*	pensieri	*thoughts*
vita	*life*	vite	*lives*
delizia	*delight*	delizie	*delights*
aria	*air*	arie	*airs*
ballata	*ballad*	ballate	*ballads*
cuore	*heart*	cuori	*hearts*
nome	*name*	nomi	*names*
tenore	*tenor*	tenori	*tenors*
madre	*mother*	madri	*mothers*

5. Using tree diagrams, show the morphemic structure of the words segmented above in question 3.

Example: prefigurazione

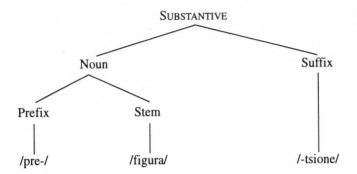

amicizia
prevedibile
incomprensibile
veramente
insincero
improbabile
sopravvivenza
summenzionato
verosimile
velocità
velocissimo
disfunzionalità
incongruo
capostazione
portalettere
attaccabrighe
verosimilitudine

6. Identify the morpheme and its allomorphs in each set of data,
   writing an appropriate distribution rule. Formulate your analysis
   solely on the basis of the data given. Do not write a complete
   morphological analysis of the category.

   a. Adjective agreement:

l'uomo bello	gli uomini belli
the handsome man	*the handsome men*
l'uomo felice	gli uomini felici
the happy man	*the happy men*

la donna bella	le donne belle
the beautiful woman	*the beautiful women*
la donna felice	le donne felici
the happy woman	*the happy women*

b. Present indicative of first-conjugation verbs:

/kantare/ → /kant-/ (verbal root)

(io)	canto	*I sing, I am singing*
(tu)	canti	*you sing, you are singing (familiar)*
(Lei)	canta	*you sing, you are singing (polite)*
(lui / lei)	canta	*he / she sings, he / she is singing*
(noi)	cantiamo	*we sing, we are singing*
(voi)	cantate	*you sing, you are singing (plural)*
(loro)	cantano	*they sing, they are singing*

c. Imperfect indicative of first-conjugation verbs:

(io)	cant*avo*	*I used to sing, I was singing*
(tu)	cant*avi*	*you used to sing, you were singing*
(Lei)	cant*ava*	*you used to sing, you were singing*
(lui/lei)	cant*ava*	*he/she used to sing, he/she was singing*
(noi)	cant*avamo*	*we used to sing, we were singing*
(voi)	cant*avate*	*you used to sing, you were singing*
(loro)	cant*avano*	*they used to sing, they were singing*

d. Demonstrative adjective of nearness:

questo libro	*this book*	*questa* notte	*this night*
questo dente	*this tooth*	*questa* luna	*this moon*
*quest'*uomo	*this man*	*quest'*isola	*this island*
questi libri	*these books*	*queste* notti	*these nights*
questi denti	*these teeth*	*queste* lune	*these moons*
questi uomini	*these men*	*queste* isole	*these islands*

e. Demonstrative adjective of farness:

quello zio	*that uncle*	*quegli* zii	*those uncles*

quel libro	*that book*	*quei* libri	*those books*
*quell'*angelo	*that angel*	*quegli* angeli	*those angels*
quella zia	*that aunt*	*quelle* zie	*those aunts*
quella penna	*that pen*	*quelle* penne	*those pens*
*quell'*isola	*that island*	*quelle* arie	*those islands*

7. Identify the suffix in each set of words, specifying predictable allomorphic variation, if any exists.

Example: disfare
disdire
disperdere
disgustare

/dis-/ = prefix
/-dis/ → [diz-] / #[+consonantal, +voiced] ... #

a.
predire
prevedere
precludere
presentire

b.
sborsare
scolorire
smettere
stendere

c.
decadere
descrivere
definire
debordare

d.
pasticcio
bisticcio
capriccio
impiccio

e.
ventiduesimo
ventitreesimo
ventottesimo
ventinovesimo

6
Sentence Patterns

....

The words of the world want to make sentences.

Gaston Bachelard (1884–1962)

Consider the following seven arrangements of the same words, all, except for one, strung together in a random fashion:

1. ragazzo il mangia pizza la
2. ragazzo pizza il la mangia
3. ragazzo pizza la il mangia
4. pizza ragazzo il la mangia
5. mangia il ragazzo pizza la
6. la il mangia ragazzo pizza
7. il ragazzo mangia la pizza

Clearly, (7) is the one that has not been put together randomly. It is the only legitimate Italian **sentence**. The other six are meaningless strings, because, even though they all consist of valid Italian words, they lack the appropriate *syntactic structure*. **Syntax** refers to the relations among words in a sentence that provide the key to deciphering its meaning. Syntactic analysis thus involves the study of how words are combined to make sentences. The term *sentence*, like the term *word*, refers to a notion that everyone intuitively knows, but which defies precise definition. This is why linguists prefer to characterize a sentence structurally as a sequence of words organized around a *subject* and a *predicate*. The **subject** is what or who the sentence is about; the predicate is what the subject does, thinks, says, or what is said, thought, indicated about the subject:

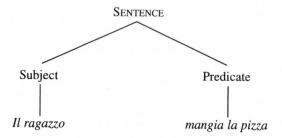

A general characteristic of sentences is that they are not constructed by a direct concatenation of single words, but rather hierarchically in terms of *phrases*. The study of syntax is, more precisely, an examination of phrase structure. In the above sentence, for instance, the subject consists of a noun phrase and the predicate of a verb phrase, which itself is made up with a verb and another noun phrase:

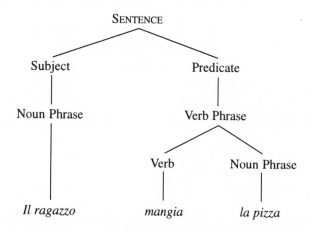

The object of this chapter is the study of how sentences are constructed. Like the previous chapter, it is impossible to carry out an in-depth investigation of this aspect of Italian here. So, we will focus on illustrating selectively how sentences in general are put together. If nothing else, it should exemplify to the reader in an explicit manner that sentences are not constructed in a linear, sequential fashion.

Phrase Structure

Expanding the segmentation technique introduced in the previous chapter for the identification of morphemic segments to include sentence segmentation, we can extrapolate the syntactic principles that make (7) the only well-formed sentence among the seven above.

First, we notice that *il* and *ragazzo* form a **syntactic category,** since the two, together, can be replaced by a proper noun, *Marco* (Prop), or a subject pronoun, *lui* (Pro), without altering the basic sentence pattern. The syntactic category to which all three belong is known as a *noun phrase* (NP):

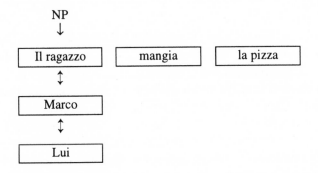

Using a tree diagram, we can show these three possibilities for NP as follows (S = sentence):

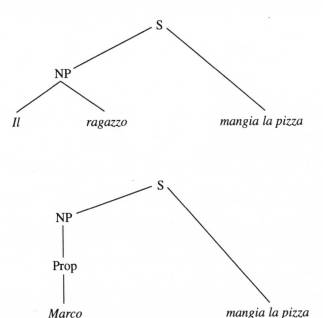

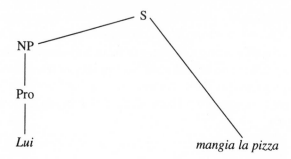

The NP *il ragazzo* can be segmented further into two categories: the *definite article* (Def) *il* and the *common noun* (N) *ragazzo*. Since the Def category can be replaced by the *indefinite article* (Indef) *un*, in the same slot, it is obvious that Def and Indef both belong to the same general category called *article* (Art). And since the *demonstrative* (Dem) – which can be realized as either the demonstrative of nearness (D1), *questo*, or the demonstrative of farness (D2), *quello* (in their allomorphically appropriate forms) – can replace Art in the same sentence slot, it is obvious that Art and Dem make up the even more general category of *determiner* (Det):

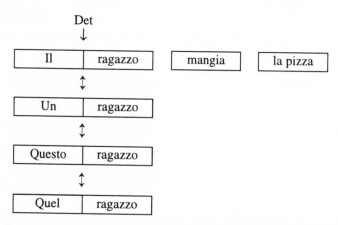

Structurally, therefore, the noun phrases *il ragazzo, un ragazzo, questo ragazzo,* and *quel ragazzo* have the same **phrase structure**. More technically, it is said that the NP category *dominates* Det + N and that Det *dominates* the categories Art and Dem.

Now, let us look at the other parts of our sentence. Since the sequence *mangia la pizza* can be replaced by *mangia* alone or by *mangia volentieri, mangia tutto,* and so on, it is evident that the whole phrase constitutes a separate syntactic category, called a *verb phrase* (VP). This particular VP consists of a verb (V) and a noun phrase which has the exact same phrase structure of the NP *il ragazzo*. Using the term *branch* to designate where categories occur on tree diagrams, it can be said, more precisely, that the NP *la pizza* is a 'right-branching' noun phrase, relative to *il ragazzo*, which is a 'left-branching' NP. In this way, a subject can be characterized as a *left-branching NP dominated by S*, and a predicate as a *right-branching NP dominated by the VP attached to S above it.*

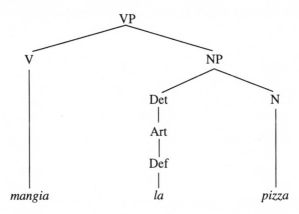

The structure of the sentence *Il ragazzo mangia la pizza* can now be shown in its entirety as follows:

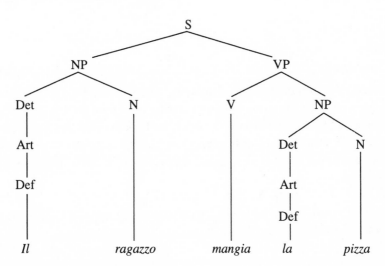

The above diagram now displays the hierarchical organization of the phrases that make up the sentence *Il ragazzo mangia la pizza* explicitly. It also makes it obvious why the other six random combinations of the same words given above are incomprehensible: they lack the phrase structure shown by the tree diagram and are thus ill formed to deliver meaning. A primary task of syntactic analysis is to determine which kinds of phrase structures exist in a given language.

For example, the sentence *Marco mangia la pasta* can be shown to have the same phrase structure at the higher nodes as *Il ragazzo mangia la pizza*. The only difference is at the level of the left-branching NP:

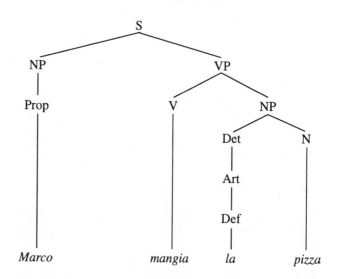

This type of analysis provides convenient 'snapshots' of the internal structure of sentences, thus displaying exactly why we feel that some sentences have the same structure and form, others do not, and others still are ill formed. However, it should be kept in mind that such 'snapshots' are simply useful procedures for relating sentences to each other; they are not snapshots of 'cognitive processes,' as some linguists have claimed.

Now, let us consider the structure of another sentence: *Tutti quei ragazzi vanno alla scuola* (Pre = predeterminer structure, PP = prepositional phrase):

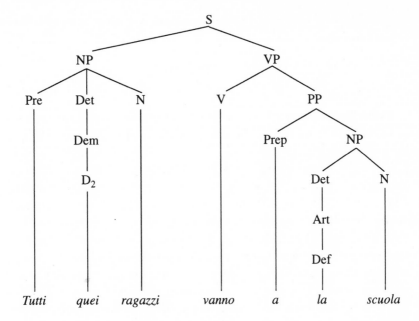

To complete the structural description of this string, it is obvious that the morphological and phonological rules of the language will have to 'kick in' at some point to refine the string, assigning it an appropriate morphological and phonological form. In this case, the /a/ + /la/ sequence in the string, for instance, would undergo syntactic doubling to produce /al:a/. This implies that the levels of language are highly intertwined: syntactic structure is dependent upon morphological structure, which, as we saw in the previous chapter, is sensitive to phonemic structure. To use a biological analogy, a sentence is like an organ that is made up of morphemic molecules, which in turn are made up of phonemic atoms. Indeed, language can be compared to an organism since it constitutes a system that can be regarded as analogous in its structure or functions to a living body.

Relations

Now consider a sentence such as *Old men and women love that program*. The relevant thing to note about this sentence is that it has potentially two meanings:

1. *Old men and women* (in general who are not necessarily old) *love that program.*

2. *Old men and old women love that program.*

These elaborations show, in effect, that the above well-formed string is ambiguous in meaning. The source of the ambiguity is that the two have different phrase structures. The second elaboration allows us to pinpoint the source of the ambiguity. The original sentence, *Old men and women love that program*, is called a **surface structure string**, whereas the unambiguous elaboration (2) is called a **deep structure string**. Now, it can be seen that the ambiguity is produced by the fact that the deep and surface structure strings are different. In the deep structure the sequence *old men and old women* has the form XY + XZ, whereas its corresponding surface structure has the form X(Y + Z), where X = old, Y = men, and Z = women. It would seem that somewhere along the line a rule akin to factorization in mathematics was applied to (2), producing the ambiguous string *Old men and women love that program*. Such a rule is called a *transformation*. The role of such a rule is, obviously, to convert deep structure strings into surface structure strings.

The task of the syntactician therefore involves determining not only phrase structure but also the relations among strings that show an isomorphic structure but convey a different meaning. The syntactician also looks for sentences, such as active and passive sentences, affirmative and negative sentences, statements and questions, and so on, that are structurally related in specific ways. Consider, for instance, the sentence *Quel libro è venduto da quel negozio*. First, we observe that it is a passive sentence. So, we start our analysis by considering its corresponding active form, *Quel negozio vende quel libro* (see top of next page).

Now let us consider the structure of the passive form: *Quel libro è venduto da quel negozio*. First, we note that the two NPs are in 'reverse position' – that is, the NP2 of the active sentence, which is in the predicate slot, is instead in the subject slot in the passive sentence. Second, the verb in the active sentence has been changed into a past tense with *essere* as the auxiliary verb. Third, the agent preposition *da* is to be inserted before NP1 in the passive form. The structure relation between

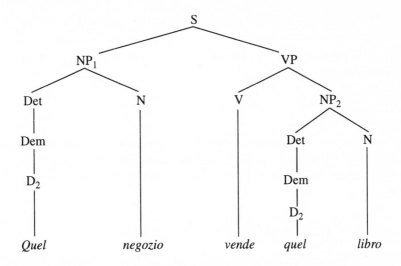

the active and passive can be formalized as follows (V[past] = past participle of the verb):

Active   Passive
NP$_1$ + V + NP$_2$ NP$_2$ + *essere* V[past] + /da/ NP$_1$

Now, consider the following sentence:

La ragazza che legge il libro è italiana

This string is really an amalgam of two simpler strings, one of which has been **embedded** into the other:

1. *La ragazza è italiana*
2. *La ragazza legge il libro*

The embedded sentence, *la ragazza legge il libro*, is known as a *clause.*

La ragazza, la ragazza legge il libro, è italiana
↓
La ragazza che legge il libro è italiana

Notice that in the embedding process the repeated subject NP is deleted and replaced by the word *che*. This constitutes a general structural feature that can be generalized as follows (NP1 = same subject noun phrase):

$$NP1 + NP1 \ldots \rightarrow NP1 + che \ldots$$

Now, since this rule can apply to any sequence of two consecutive NPs with the same subscripts, and because all relative clauses are, in effect, embedded structures, the above rule can be generalized as follows:

$$NPn + NPn \ldots \rightarrow NPn + che \ldots$$

In the above case, the embedding occurred in the subject slot of the sentence. It is thus called *left-branch embedding*. In the case of the sentence *La ragazza legge il libro che costa molto*, the embedding rule applies to NPs that branch to the right. It is thus called *right-branch embedding*. The analysis of this latter sentence will be left as an exercise below.

The Lexicon

The insertion of morphemes from a lexicon into sentence slots is called **lexical insertion**. The **lexicon** is a particular kind of dictionary that contains not only the meaning of the items, but also their syntactic specification, known as **subcategorization**. Thus, for example, the verb *mettere* would be subcategorized with the syntactic specification that must be followed by a noun phrase and a prepositional phrase (e.g., *Io metto il libro sul tavolo*). Thus, in a string that has these slots, *mettere* and other verbs like it can be put into the previous V slot in the string.

Another aspect of subcategorization is the specification of a lexical item in terms of semantic features. For instance, a noun such as *boy* is marked first and foremost as [+animate], whereas *milk* would be marked as [−animate]. If it is so marked, then it entails gender ([+male], [+female]), age ([+adult], [−adult]), and other similar specifications that keep it distinct from others in the same subcategorization domain:

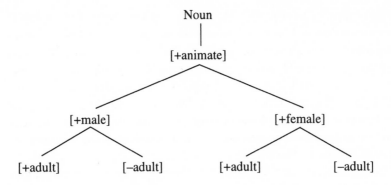

It is beyond the scope of this chapter to deal with subcategorization rules. Suffice it to say that the insertion of morphemes into the syntactic frames provided by the phrase structure of specific sentences is one that is also in part governed by rules.

Grammar and Mind

In our view, the approach to syntactic analysis illustrated above is simply a tool for showing how sentences cohere into hierarchical structures and how types of sentences are related to each other structurally. But some syntacticians claim that such rules of grammar might, in fact, be rules of mind. Noam Chomsky, for instance, has made the claim that there exists a **universal grammar** (UG) for language in the human species that has, more or less, the characteristics of the kinds of syntactic rules described schematically in this chapter.

Linguists look to the acquisition of language in childhood as indirect proof of this hypothesis. We acquire language without effort or training during our infancy. Indeed, the only requirement for learning any language, or languages, is adequate exposure to samples of it from birth to about age two. To explain the facility with which language is acquired, UG theorists claim that it is a physical organ as congenital to the human being as, say, flight is to a bird. It is the output of a set of universal grammatical principles present in the brain at birth that are subjected to culture-specific 'parameters' during infancy – the actual phrase structure rules, subcategorization rules, and so on, that characterize a specific language. The UG is thus seen as a neurological generator of syntactic principles in human beings; culture is the external force that determines which of these are relevant to the language spoken in context. This implies that all natural languages are built on the same basic neural plan and that differences are explainable as choices of rule types from a fairly small inventory of possibilities – made available to the child through environmental input. This, it is claimed, would explain the universality and rapidity of language acquisition – when the child learns one fact about a language, he or she can easily infer other facts without having to learn them one by one.

In our view, the problem with UG theory is that it is restricted to accounting for the development of a particular kind of grammar in the child. UG theory is a *theory* of syntax, not of psychobiological processes. One can make inferences between the one and the other, but there is no way to prove that the theory is 'psychologically real' in any sense of the word. Moreover, UG theory ignores the role of nonverbal factors in development (gesture, musical recognition, etc.). Since these are also developed during infancy without any training, does the brain also possess universal nonverbal grammars? If the role of culture is simply to set the parameters that determine the specific verbal grammar that develops in the child, could it not also set, say, the specific melodic and harmonic parameters that determine the specific forms of musical knowledge that develop in the child?

Another problem with UG theory is the view that syntax is built abstractly as a series of rules into the brain and is, therefore, immune to influence from the real world. The linguist Ronald Langacker has refuted this view, showing rather persuasively that certain aspects of sentence grammar are, in effect, generated by mental images that come from experience.* Consider the relation between an active and passive sentence such as *Alexander ate the apple* vs. *The apple was eaten by Alexander*. Think about what you see in your mind when saying the active sentence. The subject (*Alexander*) is in the foreground as seen by the mind's eye, while the object *(apple)* is in the background. The action implied by the verb (*eating*) is spotlighted as an activity of the subject. The overall view that active sentences convey is one of the subject as an agent, a 'perpetrator' or 'executor' of the action. A change from passive to active, however, changes the position of the foreground and the background to the mind's eye. The passive sentence brings the

---

* See his *Concept, Image, and Symbol: The Cognitive Basis of Grammar* (Berlin: Mouton de Gruyter, 1990).

apple to the foreground, relegating the eater *Alexander* to the background. The action of eating is now spotlighted on the object, the 'receiver' of the action. In effect, the passive sentence gives a different mental angle from which to see the same action.

This type of analysis suggests that sentence structures are acquired with facility, not because they are built into the brain's UG as general principles, but because they are learned by the child as perspectival tools. This is probably why sentence grammar and the ability to draw emerge in tandem in the child. Children learn early on that language allows them to model and reflect upon the world in the same way that a drawing or a melody does. Incidentally, this is perhaps why we can understand stories in virtually the same ways that we understand music or paintings. In the same fashion that a painting is much more than an assemblage of lines, shapes, colours, and melodies a combination of notes and harmonies, so too a sentence in language is much more than an assemblage of words and phrases built from some rule system in the brain. We use the grammatical elements at our disposal to model the world in ways that parallel how musicians use melodic elements and painters visual elements to model it. How and why this comes about in the human species remain a mystery.

Follow-Up Activities

1. Define the following terms and notions in your own words:

   sentence
   syntax
   subject
   syntactic category
   phrase structure
   surface structure
   deep structure
   embedding
   lexical insertion
   lexicon
   subcategorization
   universal grammar

2. Underline the noun phrases in the following text.

Example:

Verso <u>la fine</u> del <u>loro primo anno</u> di <u>vita</u> <u>i bambini</u> mostrano <u>un'abilità notevole</u> di imitare <u>i suoni linguistici</u> e <u>le parole</u> che sentono quotidianamente nel <u>loro ambiente</u>

Verso la fine del loro primo anno di vita i bambini mostrano un'abilità notevole di imitare i suoni linguistici e le parole che sentono quotidianamente nel loro ambiente. A diciotto mesi le loro parole si sono considerevolmente moltiplicate e, a questo punto, cominciano a cercare di comunicare con frasi di una, due e tre parole. All'età di tre anni i bambini dimostrano un controllo incredibile sulla percezione e sulla produzione del discorso, avendo scoperto che la capacità di parlare svolge un ruolo centrale nella vita in casa.

Quello che forse fa stupire di più è che i bambini mostrano la stessa facilità nell'apprendere più di una lingua durante il cosiddetto «periodo critico» che va dalla nascita all'età della pubertà, e cioè, durante il periodo di massima plasticità cerebrale. Da oltre un secolo molti sono stati gli studi scientifici condotti sul bilinguismo e sul plurilinguismo e molte sono state le teorie proposte allo scopo di spiegare tali fenomeni. Mentre a livello pratico, l'abilità di padroneggiare diversi codici linguistici è sempre stato considerato un attributo di grande valore, nell'ambito della scuola forse nessun'altra questione ha fatto scaturire così tante polemiche, e ha dato origine a così tante indagini scientifiche, quanto l'apprendimento e l'uso di più di una lingua per la scolarizzazione. Tali reazioni sono collegate, a parere di chi scrive, all'importanza che la società occidentale ha sempre attribuito al possesso di un singolo o dominante codice linguistico per lo sviluppo delle capacità conoscitive e per l'apprendimento delle materie scolastiche. L'uso simultaneo di un secondo e/o terzo codice, con le stesse finalità, è sempre stato, per contro, considerato una fonte potenziale d'interferenza nella formazione linguistica e conoscitiva del bambino. Le indagini psicologiche costituiscono un punto di partenza particolarmente importante per convalidare la fondatezza psicologica di un'educazione bilingue.

3. Specify the phrase structure of the following sentences using tree diagrams. Identify any new symbol (e.g., Adv = adverb) that you might need.

Example: Quel ragazzo gioca volentieri.

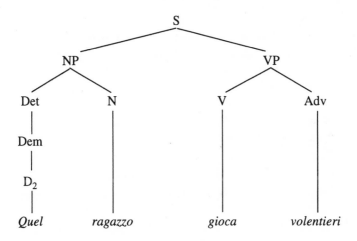

   a. La madre di Gilda è americana
   b. Maria è una donna veramente intelligente
   c. Quegli amici vanno sempre al cinema insieme
   d. Tutti vogliono andare in Italia quest'anno
   e. Anche tu guardi la televisione ogni sera.
   f. Claudia telefona a Marco.
   g. La madre di Gilda è americana
   h. Maria è una donna veramente intelligente
   i. Quegli amici vanno sempre al cinema insieme
   j. Tutti vogliono andare in Italia quest'anno
   k. Anche tu guardi la televisione ogni sera.

4. Each of the following sentences is ambiguous. Decode its meanings by giving its various potential deep structure forms.

Example: Ci vuole
            1. (Lui/lei) vuole noi
            2. È necessario

   a. Ci vediamo
   b. Non ci va
   c. Ci conta

5. Analyse the following sentences, as best you can, in relative-structural terms.

Example   I bambini non vanno a scuola oggi.
This sentence is a negative form of *I bambini vanno a scuola.*
The negative form in Italian has the general structure:
NP1 + V ... → NP1 + *non* + V ...

   a. Non tutti gli studenti amano quel corso.
   b. Chiamano quel professore, gli studenti?
   c. Questo è un quadro di Modigliani, vero?
   d. La lezione è stata fatta da un altro insegnante.
   e. Marco e Claudia non studiano né il francese né il tedesco, ma l'italiano.
   f. La ragazza legge il libro che costa molto.
   g. Quel ragazzo è la persona che ho visto ieri.
   h. Tutti sanno che tu vuoi tornare in Italia.
   i. Il ragazzo che guarda la televisione che abbiamo comprato ieri è il cugino che è venuto ieri dall'Italia.

6. Discuss the validity of the notion of universal grammar.

7
Meaning

....

For a large class of cases – though not for all – in which we employ the word 'meaning' it can be defined thus: the meaning of a word is its use in the language.

Ludwig Wittgenstein (1889–1951)

In previous chapters we have been dissecting sounds, syllables, words, phrases, and sentences, on the basis of differentiations in *meaning*. However, we did not define what *meaning* is. Like the terms *word* or *sentence*, meaning is something that people also intuitively understand but that defies precise definition.

The purpose of this chapter is to look more closely at meaning in itself. The study of this aspect of language goes under the rubric of **semantics**. While the areas of linguistic study covered in the previous chapters were concerned primarily with the structure and form of linguistic elements, semantics is the branch that deals with the meaning of those elements. Again, it is impossible to give an in-depth treatment of semantic phenomena in a single chapter. So, we will limit the discussion to illustrating what kinds of topics a basic semantic analysis would embrace.

Words as Signs

We start by observing that every word, phrase, or sentence is a sign. A **sign** is anything – a word, a gesture, an utterance, and so on – that stands for something other than itself. The word *gatto*, for instance, is a sign because it does not stand for the phonemes that comprise it, /gat:o/, but rather for 'a carnivorous mammal (*Felis catus*) domesticated since early times as a catcher of rats and mice.' Similarly, an open hand directed at a person is a sign because it does not stand for itself, the hand, but rather for a warning motion alerting someone to stop. The 'something other than itself' that the sign stands for is called the refer-ent:

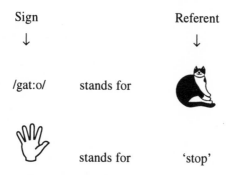

Sign		Referent
↓		↓

/gat:o/   stands for

stands for   'stop'

More technically, the physical form of the sign (e.g., the combina-tion of phonemes) is called the **signifier**, and the concept to which it refers, the **signified** or **referent**. There are two kinds of referents that signs designate, concrete and abstract:

1. A *concrete* referent, such as the physical colour designated by the word *azzurro*, is something existing in reality or in real experience and is, normally, perceptible by the senses.
2. An *abstract* referent, such as *un'idea brillante*, is something that is formed in the mind.

The sign is a powerful mental tool because it allows its users to con-jure up the things to which it refers even though these might not be physically present for the senses to perceive. This feature of signs is known psychologically as **displacement**. By simply uttering the word *gatto*, people understand what is being singled out in the world of ex-perience, even though an actual 'cat' may not be present for people to observe. Similarly, by simply saying the expression *un'idea brillante*, people will understand what is being implied, even though no such thing is available for the senses to detect. This remarkable feature of signs has endowed the human species with the ability to refer to any-thing at will, even to something that is made up completely by human fancy.

The relation that holds between the physical form of the sign (the signifier) and its referent (the signified) is known as **signification**. The meaning of a word or phrase can now be specified more technically as its *signification*. This entails all the possible uses (signifieds) of the sign. Take, for example, the English word *cat*. Some of its referents are as follows:

1. a small carnivorous mammal domesticated since early times as a catcher of rats and mice and as a pet and existing in several distinctive breeds and varieties;
2. a person, especially a male player or devotee of jazz music, as in *He's a cool cat*;
3. a secret, as in *He let the cat out of the bag*.

These show that there are several types of meaning in word signification. The first definition constitutes what is commonly known as *literal*, or more accurately, *denotative* meaning. The second shows that a word's meaning can be extended to encompass other referents that are seen to have something in common with cats. This type of meaning is known as *connotative*. The third reveals that a word's meaning can be used **figuratively**. We will look at all three types in this chapter. At this point it is sufficient to note that deciphering the meaning of words and other structures is hardly a simple process. Determining what kind of meaning a sign has entails knowing: (1) the purely denotative aspects of the sign; (2) the pragmatic or contextual conditions that hold between speakers and signs; and (3) the syntactic aspects, in which formal relations among the elements within signs (for example, among the sounds in a sentence) are indicated.

The pragmatic aspect of a sign's meaning requires some commentary here. The British philosopher J.L. Austin claimed in his 1962 book *How to Do Things with Words* (Harvard University Press) that, by speaking, a person performs an *act* (such as state, predict, or warn), and that the meaning of the act is to be found in what it brings about. The American philosopher John R. Searle extended Austin's ideas in the 1970s, emphasizing the need to relate the functions of speech acts to their social context. Searle asserted that speech encompasses at least three kinds of acts:

1. **locutionary acts**, in which things are said with a certain sense (as in *La luna è una sfera*);

2. **illocutionary acts**, in which something has been promised or ordered to be acted out (as in *Lo farò, prima o poi; Vieni qui!* etc.); and

3. **perlocutionary acts**, in which the speaker, by speaking, does something to someone else, for example, angers, consoles, persuades someone (as in *Mi dispiace, Non ti preoccupare, Dai, dimmi tutto!* etc.).

The speaker's intentions are conveyed by the force that is given to the speech act. To be successfully interpreted, however, the words used must also be appropriate, sincere, consistent with the speaker's general beliefs and conduct, and recognizable as meaningful by the hearer.

Denotation and Connotation

The two primary kinds of meaning that a sign can have, denotative and connotative, also depend on usage and situation. **Denotation** is the initial referent a sign captures. But the referent is not something specific in the world, but rather a prototypical exemplar of a *category*. For instance, the word *gatto* does not refer to a specific 'cat,' although it can, but to an exemplar of the category of animals that we recognize as having the quality 'catness.' The denotative meaning of *cat* is, therefore, really 'a creature exemplifying *catness*.' The mental concept that this entails is, therefore, marked by generic distinctive semantic features such as [+mammal], [+retractile claws], [+long tail], etc. This composite mental picture allows us to determine if a specific real or imaginary animal under consideration will fall within the category of *catness*. Similarly, the word *square* does not denote a specific 'square,' but rather a figure consisting of four equal straight lines that meet at right angles. It is irrelevant if the lines are thick, dotted, two metres long, or whatever. So long as the figure can be seen to have the distinctive features [+four equal straight lines] and [+meeting at right angles], it is identifiable denotatively as a square.

Now, the meaning of a sign can be extended freely to encompass other kinds of referents that appear, by association or analogy, to have something in common with the original referent. This extensional process is known as **connotation**. The meaning of *cat* as a jazz musician is an example of how connotation works – the jazz musician is perceived to move slowly, sleekly, and rhythmically to slow jazz music, like the mammal called a *cat*.

As another example, consider the word *house*. This word denotes, more or less, 'any (free-standing) structure intended for human habitation.' This meaning can be seen in utterances such as *I bought a new house yesterday, House prices are continually going up in this city, We repainted our house the other day*, and so on. Now, note that the same word can be extended connotatively as follows:

1. The *house* is in session = *legislative assembly*
2. The *house* roared with laughter = *audience in a theatre*
3. They sleep at one of the *houses* at Harvard University = *dormitory*

However, such extensions of the word are hardly random or disconnected to its original meaning. Rather, the semantic features that make up its denotative meaning – [+structure], [+human], [+habitation] – are implicit in such extensional uses; that is, a legislative assembly, a theatre audience, and a dormitory do indeed imply *structures* of special kinds that *humans* can be said to *inhabit* (occupy) in some specific way. Any connotative extension of the word *house* is thus constrained by the distinctive features of its meaning; that is, *house* can be applied to refer to anything that involves or implicates humans (or beings) coming together for some specific reason. More formally, connotation can be defined as the mapping of the semantic features of a word onto a new referent, if it is perceived to entail these features by association or analogy.

There is another type of connotation that is worth mentioning here. It is called *emotive*. The word *sì*, for example, can have various emotive connotations, depending on the tone of voice with which it is uttered. If one says it with a normal tone of voice, it will be understood as a sign of affirmation. If, however, one says it with a raised tone, as in a question, *sì?*, then it would imply doubt or incredulity. Such 'added meanings' to the word *yes* are examples of emotive connotation.

The distinction between denotative and connotative meanings is the key principle used in the making of dictionaries – known as the science of **lexicography**. The primary task in lexicography is to unravel the semantic features that constitute a word's fundamental meaning – its denotation – and from which all other meanings can be derived – its connotations.

The technique of identifying the semantic features that are needed to specify denotative meanings can be illustrated with the following example. Consider the words below:

1. *padre, madre, figlio, figlia*

2. *bue, mucca, vitello, vitella*

3. *cane, cagna, cagnolino, cagnolina*

If we contrast these items with words such as *pane, latte, spada, auto,* and so on. we can easily see that they all share the property of animacy. Hence, the feature [±animate] would appear to be a basic one in establishing the denotative meaning of items. Now, comparing the items in (1) with those in (2) and (3), it is easy to see that they are kept distinct by the feature [±human]; and comparing (2) and (3) reveals the need of further distinctions, [±bovine] and [±canine]. Within each category, what keeps the first two separate from the second two is the feature [±adult]. Finally, [±male] and [±female] are needed to ensure that all items contrast by at least one feature.

This type of analysis is parallel to the distinctive-feature approach used in phonological analysis (Chapter 4). We can draw up a similar type of chart to the ones we drew up in Chapter 4 to show which distinctive semantic features are possessed by each word as follows:

	Animate	Human	Bovine	Canine	Adult	Male	Female
PADRE	+	+	−	−	+	+	−
MADRE	+	+	−	−	+	−	+
FIGLIO	+	+	−	−	−	+	−
FIGLIA	+	+	−	−	−	−	+
BUE	+	−	+	−	+	+	−
MUCCA	+	−	+	−	+	−	+
VITELLO	+	−	+	−	−	+	−
VITELLA	+	−	+	−	−	−	+
CANE	+	−	−	+	+	+	−
CAGNA	+	−	−	+	+	−	+
CAGNOLINO	+	−	−	+	−	+	−
CAGNOLINA	+	−	−	+	−	−	+

This type of analysis makes it possible to show what differentiates, say, *madre* from *figlia* or *vitella* from *cagna*. Here are some minimal contrasts:

padre ~ *madre*
[+male] ~ [+female]

padre ~ figlio
[+adult] ~ [–adult]

vitella ~ cagna
[+bovine] ~ [–bovine]
or
[–canine] ~ [+canine]

cane ~ cagnolina
[+adult] ~ [–adult]
and
[+male] ~ [+female]

As in the case of phonetic distinctive features, there are also some redundancies in the assignment of semantic features. Here are two of them:

- If an item possesses the feature [+human], then it also possesses [+animate].
- If an item possesses the feature [+male], then it also possesses the feature [–female].

Although this is a useful way of establishing the denotative meaning of lexical items, it can produce anomalous results. The opposition above between *vitella* and *cagna* can be given as either [+bovine] ~ [–bovine] or [–canine] ~ [+canine]. There really is no way to establish which one is, psychologically, the actual trigger in the opposition. Moreover, when certain words are defined in terms of features, it becomes obvious that to keep them distinct one will need a vast array of semantic features. The whole exercise would thus become artificial and convoluted.

One way to avoid the latter problem is to group words that share one or more features together into what are known as **lexical fields**. For example, one such field is that of colours, which all share the feature [+chromatic].

arancione	*orange*
azzurro	*blue*
bianco	*white*

blu	*dark blue*
celeste	*light blue*
giallo	*yellow*
grigio	*grey*
marrone	*brown*
nero	*black*
rosso	*red*
verde	*green*
viola	*violet, purple*
etc.	

Now, distinguishing between individual items will depend on what wavelength a specific word denotes. The opposition is thus no longer one that involves feature differentiation, but rather degree. In essence, lexical fields are characterized by the distinctive semantic features that differentiate the individual lexemes in the field from one another, and also by features shared by all the lexemes in the field. For example, items that have the feature [+seat] (i.e., 'something on which to sit'), such as *sedia, sofà, banco, panca*, obviously belong to the same lexical field. Within the field they can be distinguished from one another according to how many people are accommodated and whether a back support is included.

Research on identifying a universal set of such semantic features is ongoing, but it has yet to yield a manageable set of features. The theoretical problem that this poses has proven to be quite intractable. Unlike phonological subsystems, which are closed, semantic systems are open-ended and constantly changing to meet new social needs. This makes it virtually impossible to develop a core set of features for describing them.

Semantic Relations

Another technique linguists use to determine how words bear meaning is by comparing words in terms of how they relate to each other. One such relation is that of *synonymy*. **Synonyms** are words having the same or nearly the same meaning in one or more senses: for example, *vicino–appresso, lontano–distante*, and so on. However, there is virtually never a case of pure synonymy. Take, for instance, *piacere* and *essere simpatico*. Ignoring nuances of meaning for the sake of argument, we can see that the following sentences are interpretable as virtually synonymous:

Tu mi piaci	↔	*Tu mi sei simpatico*
Lei mi piace	↔	*Lei mi è simpatica*

The difference in meaning between the two is one of degree: *mi piaci* is stronger in sentiment than *mi sei simpatico*. However, when referring denotatively to referents marked [–animate], then only *piacere* can be used: *Mi piace la pizza,* but not *Mi è simpatica la pizza.* This shows that the two do not completely overlap in range of application and are thus not pure synonyms.

The counterpart of synonymy is *antonymy.* **Antonyms** are words that are opposite in meaning: *notte* vs. *giorno, triste* vs. *felice, freddo* vs. *caldo, bene* vs. *male,* and so forth. But antonymy, like synonymy, is a matter of degree, rather than of categorical difference. One way to show this is to consider antonyms as extreme points on a continuum, and to allocate items and structures in between these two end points. Thus, in between *giorno* and *notte* one would find concepts such as *pomeriggio, sera, buio,* and so on.

Another semantic relation is that of *homonymy.* **Homonyms** are words or phrases with the same pronunciation and/or spelling, but with different meanings. If the homonymy is purely phonetic, then the items are known as **homophones** (e.g., *aunt* vs. *ant* and *bore* vs. *boar*). If the homonymy is orthographic, then the words are known as **homographs** (*play* as in *Shakespeare's play* vs. *play* as in *He likes to play*). It is not the case that all homographs are homophones: for example, the form *learned* has two pronunciations in (1) *He learned to play the violin* vs. (2) *He is a learned man.*

A fourth type of relation that words have with each other is known as **hyponymy**, the process by which the meaning of one sign is included in that of another: e.g., the meaning of *scarlet* is included in the meaning of *red,* the meaning of *tulipano* is included in that of *fiore*, and so forth.

Utterances

As we saw in the previous chapter, sentence meaning is not the sum of the meanings of the individual words. Indeed, there seems to be a close relation between sentence structure and the words used in making sentences. For instance, the position of the adjective with respect to the noun will sometimes entail a difference in meaning:

BEFORE	AFTER
Lui è un grande amico	Lui è un amico grande
He's a great friend	*He's a big friend*
Lui è un povero uomo	Lui è un uomo povero
He's a poor (destitute) man	*He's a poor (indigent) man*

This implies that word meaning is not impervious to syntactic structure. To unravel how the words in sentences and utterances bear meaning, linguists have established the technique of classifying them simultaneously into *expression classes* (classes of items that can substitute for one another) and *syntactic classes* (such as nouns and verbs). This allows the analyst to determine what kinds of grammatical functions a word performs and how it bears meaning in relation to other words in phrases and sentences. For example, *baciare* belongs to an expression class with other items such as *battere* and *vedere* as well as to the syntactic category *Transitive Verb*, making it appropriate only in syntactic strings that show a subject and direct object as part of their structural make-up.

The most crucial aspect in determining utterance meaning, however, is not some internal syntactic criterion but, more often than not, the external *context*. This is the real-world condition or situation that constrains what an utterance means. Consider the sentence *The pig is ready to eat*. This has at least three meanings that are determined by the separate social contexts in which it is uttered:

1. If uttered by a farmer during feeding time, the word *pig* will assume denotative meaning, and hence be marked purely as [+swine].
2. If uttered by a cook who is announcing the fact that she or he has finished cooking pork meat which is thus available for consumption, then the word *pig* is marked as [+swine] and [+cooked].
3. If uttered critically by a person to describe someone who appears to be gluttonous and to have a ravenous appetite, then the feature [+swine] has been extended connotatively to encompass a referent that possesses the feature [+human].

Clearly, utterance meaning depends in large part on the situational context in which a sentence is formed. Such contextual phenomena have, until recently, been considered to be separate from internal syntactic and semantic structure. But, as work on communication has shown, it is virtually impossible to separate purely *linguistic competence* (knowledge of phonology, morphology, syntax, and semantics) from *communicative competence* (knowledge of how to make words and sentences bear meanings in specific situations).

Names

The semantic system of a language is both an 'inward' and 'outward' branching system. By inward we mean simply that it has roots 'within' the overall linguistic system, as we have seen; by outward we mean that it links a language to the outside world of reality, and especially to the community that uses it for functional purposes.

As a practical example of the latter, consider the phenomenon of *naming*. A **name** identifies a person in relation to other persons; it is a product of historical forces and thus tied to conventional systems of signification. Less often, names are coined descriptively. Trivial but instructive examples of this can be seen in the names we give household animals – *Ruff, Purry,* and so on.

The study of names falls under the branch of linguistics called **onomastics** (from Greek *onoma,* 'name'). The phenomenon of name giving in the human species is indeed a fascinating one on many counts. Across cultures, a neonate is not considered a full-fledged member of the culture until he is given a name. The act of naming a newborn infant is his first rite of passage in society, becoming identified as a separate individual with a unique personality. If a person is not given a name by her family, then society will step in to do so. A person taken into a family, by marriage, adoption, or for some other reason, is also typically assigned the family's name. From childhood on, the individual's sense of self is felt somehow to be embedded in her name. In Inuit cultures, for instance, an individual is perceived to have a body, a soul, and a name; a person is not seen as complete without all three.

In Western culture, the Judaeo-Christian influence on first names has been especially strong. In some countries, like Brazil, a child must be given an appropriate Christian name before he or she can be issued a birth certificate. Although this might seem like an extreme measure, name giving is constrained by traditions and conventions in all cultures. In Western culture, generally, name giving is a much more open and unregulated process. But even in the West, it is shaped by several customs and trends – for example, modern names often are derived from sources such as the names of the months (*Gennaro*), popular contemporary personalities (*Walter*), flowers (*Margherita*), places (*Olimpia*), or figures in classical myth (*Diana, Omero*).

Until the late Middle Ages, one personal name was generally sufficient as an identifier in Italy. Duplications, however, began to occur so often that additional differentiations became a necessity. Hence, *cognomi* ('surnames') were given to individuals. These either identified the individual in terms of place or parentage (descendancy) or else referred to some personal or social feature (e.g., occupation) of the individual. Thus, for example, a person living near or in the city of Pisa would be called *Lorenzo da Pisa* ('Lorenzo from Pisa') or *Lorenzo Pisano*. Such regional or place identifiers (*Bosco, Prato,* etc.) constitute a productive source of Italian surnames. Descendant identifiers were coined typically with the preposition *di*: *Marco Di Maria* ('Marco, [son] of Mary'), *Rinaldo De Luca*, ('Rinaldo [son] of Luca or the Lucas'), and so on. The final vowel /-i/, a genitive marker in older versions of the language, was also used to designate the individual's lineage: for example, *Michele Bassani* ('Michele [son] of Bassano'). Identifiers reflecting medieval life and occupations were also used productively to surname people: *Fabbro, Martelli,* and so on. And, last but not least, some people were identified in terms of some physical or social characteristic: *Rosetti, Bellini, Porcelli,* and so forth.

As these examples show, name-giving is both interconnected to the other systems of the language (phonological, morphological, etc.) and also with the outer world of custom, usage, and necessity. In naming people, we link them simultaneously to a language system and to the community that uses that system to carry out its social and personal needs.

Metaphor

Recall from above the third meaning of *cat*, namely its figurative meaning in *He let the cat out of the bag*. In traditional semantic approaches, this type of meaning, called **metaphorical**, has been considered to be a matter of ornamental style, rather than a feature of predictable semantic structure. However, since the late 1970s this view has changed radically. Many semanticists now see figurative meaning as systematic and regular.

Defining metaphor poses an interesting dilemma. In the metaphor *Il professore è una serpe,* there are two referents, not one, that are related to each other:

- There is the primary referent, *il professore*, which is known as the **topic** of the metaphor.
- Then there is another referent, *la serpe*, which is known as the **vehicle** of the metaphor.
- Their correlation creates a new meaning, called the **ground**, which is not the simple sum of the meanings of the two referents.

It is not the denotative meaning of the vehicle that is transferred to the topic, but rather its connotations, namely the characteristics perceived in snakes – 'slyness,' 'danger,' 'slipperiness,' and so forth. It is this complex of connotations that is associated with the topic.

Metaphor reveals a basic tendency of the human mind to think of certain referents (the topic of the metaphor) in terms of others (the vehicle). The question now becomes: Is there any psychological motivation for this? In the case of *Il professore è una serpe*, the probable reason for correlating two semantically unrelated referents seems to be the de facto perception that humans and animals are interconnected in the natural scheme of things.

The linguist George Lakoff and the philosopher Mark Johnson were the first modern-day scholars to show, in their groundbreaking book of 1980, *Metaphors We Live By*, how metaphorical meanings constitute an integral part of semantic systems and are not just a device of poets and orators. First, Lakoff and Johnson assert what Aristotle – the discoverer of metaphor, who coined this term (*meta*, 'across' + *pherein*, 'to bear') – claimed two millennia before, namely that there are two types of concepts – concrete and abstract. But the two scholars add a remarkable twist to the Aristotelian distinction, namely that abstract concepts constitute the topics of metaphors and that these are 'explained' systematically by concrete vehicles through metaphorical reasoning.

Lakoff and Johnson refer to abstract concepts as **conceptual metaphors**. These are generalized metaphorical formulas that define specific abstractions. For example, the expression *Il professore è una serpe* is really a token of something more general, namely, [people are animals]. We will put these 'general referents' in square brackets to indicate that they are minimal units of meaning. This is why we say that *Giovanni* or *Maria* or whoever is a *serpe, maiale, aquila*, and so on. Each specific metaphor (*Giovanni è un maiale, Maria è un'aquila*, etc.) is not an isolated example of poetic fancy. It is really a manifestation of a more general metaphorical idea: [people are animals].

Each of the two parts of the conceptual metaphor is called a *domain*: [people] is called the **target domain** because it is the abstract topic itself (the 'target' of the conceptual metaphor); and [animals] is called the **source domain** because it encompasses the class of vehicles that deliver the metaphor (the 'source' of the metaphorical concept). An *abstract concept* can now be defined simply as a 'mapping' of the concrete source domain onto the abstract target domain. This model suggests that abstract concepts are formed systematically through such mappings and that specific metaphors are traced to the target and source domains. So, when we hear people talking, for instance, of 'ideas' in terms of geometrical figures and relations – *Quelle idee sono parallele, sono diametralmente opposte, sono tangenziali*, and so forth – we can now easily identify the two domains as [ideas] (= target domain) and [geometrical figures/relations] (= source domain) and, therefore, the conceptual metaphor as [ideas are geometrical figures/relations].

Lakoff and Johnson trace the psychological source of conceptual metaphors to *image schemas*. These are the mental links between experiences of concrete things (like geometrical figures) and abstract concepts (like ideas). These schemas not only permit us to recognize patterns, but also to anticipate certain consequences and to make inferences and deductions. Schemas are mental maps that can reduce a large quantity of sensory information into general patterns. Image schema theory suggests that the source domains enlisted in delivering an abstract topic are not chosen in an arbitrary fashion, but derived from the experience of events. The formation of a conceptual metaphor, therefore, is the result of an experiential induction.

Lakoff and Johnson identify three types of image schemas. The first one involves mental *orientation*. This underlies concepts that are derived from our physical experiences of orientation – *up vs. down, back vs. front, near vs. far*, and so on. This produces conceptual metaphors like [happiness is up] (*Oggi mi sento su di morale*). The second type involves *ontological* thinking. This produces conceptual metaphors in which activities, emotions, ideas, etc. are associated with entities and substances: for example, [the mind is a container] (*Sono pieno zeppo di belle memorie*). The third type of schema is an elaboration of the other two. This produces *structural metaphors* that distend orientational and ontological concepts: for example, the concept [time is a resource] is built from [time is a resource] and [time is a quantity] (*Il mio tempo ti costerà molto*). Here is just a sampling of how image schemas produce various concepts:

[happiness is up/sadness is down]

- Oggi mi sento *su* di morale.
- Lei, invece si sente *giù*.

[knowledge is light/ignorance is darkness]

- Quel libro mi ha *illuminato*.
- Quello che ha detto *ha gettato luce* sulla questione.
- Quella è un'idea molto *chiara*.
- La sua teoria è *oscura*.

[ideas are food]

- Ciò che disse mi lasciò un *sapore amaro* in bocca.
- Ci sono troppi fatti qui perché io li possa *digerire* tutti.
- È un lettore *vorace*.
- Non abbiamo bisogno di *imboccare* i nostri studenti.
- Quell'idea ha *fermentato* per anni.

[ideas are people]

- È il *padre* della biologia moderna.
- Quelle idee medioevali *vivono* ancora.
- La psicologia cognitiva è ancora nella sua *infanzia*.
- Quell'idea dovrebbe essere fatta *risorgere*.
- *Alitò* nuova vita in quell'idea.

[ideas are fashion]

- Quell'idea è andata *fuori moda* anni fa.
- Berkeley è un centro del pensiero di *avanguardia*.
- L'idea di rivoluzione non è più in *voga*.

- Le idee derivate dall'informatica sono divenute proprio *chic*.

We do not detect the presence of image schemas in such common expressions because of their repeated usage.

The last relevant point made by Lakoff and Johnson in their truly fascinating book is that cultural groupthink is built on conceptual metaphors. This is accomplished by a kind of 'higher-order' metaphorizing. As target domains are associated with many kinds of source domains, the concepts become increasingly more complex, leading to what Lakoff and Johnson call **cultural**, or *cognitive*, **models**. To see what this means, consider the target domain of *sport talk*. The following source domains, among many others, underlie a large portion of discourse about sports:

[fortune]

- Quella squadra è *fortunata*.
- La loro vincita è *imprevedibile*.

[war]

- Quella squadra è stata *sconfitta*.
- Quella squadra ha un buon *attacco* e una buona *tattica*.
- Quella partita è stata una *battaglia*.

[game playing]

- Che bella *mossa*!
- Quella squadra *ha centrato*.

[economics]

- Quella squadra ha *incassato* un bel gol.
- Quel giocatore *ha pagato* il gol con un infortunio.

[eating]

- Quella squadra ha *fame* di vincere.
- Loro sono *digiuni* di vittorie.

[science]

• Sono giocatori *sperimentati*.
• Quella squadra gioca con precisione *geometrica*.

[thought system]

• Hanno un'ottima *filosofia* di gioco.
• Quella squadra ha finalmente sviluppato una *mentalità* vincente.

The constant juxtaposition of such source domains in common discourse produces, cumulatively, what is called a cultural model of sports. Before Lakoff and Johnson's trend-setting work, the study of metaphor fell within the field of *rhetoric*, where it was viewed as one of various *tropes* – that is, figures of speech. But since the early 1980s the practice has been to use the term *metaphor* to refer to the study of all figurative language and to consider the other tropes as particular kinds of metaphor. Within this framework, personification, for instance (*Il mio gatto parla inglese*), would be seen as a particular kind of metaphor, one in which the target domain is an animal or inanimate object and the source domain a set of vehicles that are normally associated with human beings (the opposite of the [people are animals] concept, namely [animals are people]). The same kind of reasoning is now applied to most of the other classical tropes. These are the result of a 'mapping' operation of elements from a source domain to a target domain.

Two types of rhetorical figures are regularly considered separately from metaphor: metonymy and irony. **Metonymy** involves the use of an entity to refer to another that is related to it. Unlike metaphor, it entails the use of a part of a domain to represent the whole domain:

• A lei piace il Dostoyevski (= the writings of Dostoyevski).
• Mia madre odia i blue jeans (= i.e., the fact that I am wearing them).
• L'automobile sta rovinando la salute (= the collection of automobiles).
• Quante facce ci sono nel pubblico (= people)
• Non ci piacciono i capelloni (= people with long hair)
• Ho comprato una FIAT (= car named FIAT)
• Gli autobus sono in sciopero (= bus drivers)
• La Chiesa è contro l'infedeltà (= Catholic theologians, priests, etc.)

- La Casa Bianca non dice niente in proposito (= the president, the American government)

Irony is the use of words to convey a meaning contrary to their literal sense – for example, *Amo essere torturato.* It allows someone to make a comment on a situation without any personal stake or involvement in it. As such, it is both a protective strategy, deflecting attention away from the self towards others by which one can make value judgments of others without commitment, and a verbal weapon that can be used aggressively towards others.

Follow-Up Activities

1. Define the following terms and notions in your own words.

   semantics
   sign
   signifier
   signified
   referent
   displacement
   signification
   figurative meaning
   locutionary act
   illocutionary act
   perlocutionary act
   denotation
   connotation
   lexicography
   lexical field
   synonym
   antonym
   homonym
   homophone
   homograph
   hyponymy
   name
   onomastics
   metaphor

topic
vehicle
ground
conceptual metaphor
target domain
source domain
name
onomastics
cultural model
metonymy
irony

2. For the following words, indicate the signifier and the signified.

   Example: gatto
   signifier = /gá-t:o/
   signified = a carnivorous mammal (*Felis catus*) domesticated since early times as a catcher of rats and
   mice

   tavolo
   uomo
   donna
   idea
   amore
   vigliacco
   furbo
   camminare
   prendere
   volentieri
   bene

3. In the following sets of expressions, indicate whether the meaning
   of the italicized word is denotative, connotative, or figurative.

   Example: Il mio *gatto* è siamese = *denotative*
   In quest'aula ci sono quattro *gatti* = *connotative*
   Quando il *gatto* non c'è, i topi ballano = *figurative*

a. Ci sono due belle *finestre* nel mio salotto.
   È uscito dalla porta e rientrato dalla *finestra.*
   Spediscila in una busta a *finestra.*

b. Hanno portato al *cielo* le sue doti personali e professionali.
   Per amor del *cielo*!
   Sono al settimo *cielo.*

c. Apri la *porta*!
   Questo mi ha aperto la *porta* del successo.
   Apri la *porta* del frigo!

4. Identify each utterance as locutionary, illocutionary, or perlocutionary.

   Example: Vieni qui!
   perlocutionary

   Veramente?
   Non è vero.
   La mia amica vive in Italia.
   Dimmi tutto quello che sai.
   Zitto!
   Che ore sono?
   Mi chiamo Alessandro.
   Sara, non ti preoccupare.
   Sarò io a farlo.
   Anche tu capisci lo spagnolo?

5. Establish the least number of semantic features that will be needed to keep each set of words distinct.

   Example: ragazzo
                ragazza
                uomo
                donna

	ragazzo	ragazza	uomo	donna
[adult]	–	–	+	+
[male]	+	–	+	–
[female]	–	+	–	+

a.

la bocca	*mouth*
il braccio	*arm*
i capelli	*hair (on the head)*
il collo	*neck*
il corpo	*body*
il dito	*finger*
la faccia	*face*
la fronte	*forehead*
la gamba	*leg*
il ginocchio	*knee*
il gomito	*elbow*
la guancia	*cheek*
il labbro	*lip*
la lingua	*tongue*
la mano	*hand*
il naso	*nose*
l'occhio	*eye*
l'orecchio	*ear*
il petto	*chest*
il piede	*foot*
la spalla	*shoulder*
la testa	*head*
l'unghia	*fingernail*

b.

la madre	*mother*
il padre	*father*
il figlio	*son*
la figlia	*daughter*
il fratello	*brother*
la sorella	*sister*
il nonno	*grandfather*
la nonna	*grandmother*
lo zio	*uncle*
la zia	*aunt*
il cugino	*cousin (male)*
la cugina	*cousin (female)*

6. Indicate whether the following pairs of items are synonyms, antonyms, homonyms, or hyponyms.

Example   bianco – nero
            antonyms

felice – contento
brutto – bello
toro – animale
figlio – famiglia
sempre – mai
moto – vettura
davanti – di fronte

7. Determine the differences in meaning between *sapere* and *conoscere*.

sapere	*conoscere*
Violetta sa che cosa è la follia.	Violetta conosce Alfredo.
Violetta knows what folly is.	*Violetta knows Alfredo.*
Alfredo sa godersi la vita.	Alfredo conosce il mondo.
Alfredo knows how to enjoy life.	*Alfredo knows the world.*

8. Identify the source from which the following names are derived.

Examples: Fiorella
              flowers

Giovanni
Maria
Alessandro
Sara
Elio
Tiberio
Violetta
Bianca

9. Identify the source of the following surnames.

   Examples: Cortese = *descriptive*
   Di Mauro = *lineage (parentage)*
   Lucchese = *topographical (place)*

   Da Vinci
   Pavese
   Alighieri
   Buonarroti
   Cardinale
   De Felice
   Verdi
   Rossini
   Paganini
   Martini
   Bellini
   Magri
   Baldo
   Siciliano

10. In the following metaphorical utterances identify the topics and
    the vehicles. Then paraphrase the ground (meaning) of each.

    Example: Maria è una salame.
    Topic = Maria
    Vehicle = rosa
    Ground = Maria is very beautiful (as a rose is).

    Lui è un salame.
    Maria è una volpe.
    La mia casa è una tana.
    Il mio computer è un gioiello.
    La mia vita è un inferno.

11. Give the conceptual metaphor that underlies each set of state-
    ments.

Example: Lui ha un cervello elettronico.
La mia mente oggi non funziona.
Ho perso la memoria.
Conceptual Metaphor: [the mind is a machine]

a.
Le vostre tesi sono indifendibili.
Attaccò ogni punto debole nella mia discussione.
Non ho mai vinto una discussione con lui.
Non sei d'accordo? Okay, spara.
Ha sparato a zero su tutti i miei argomenti.

b.
La nostra è un'amicizia profonda.
La loro amicizia è altolocata.
La nostra amicizia non è superficiale.

c.
Il nostro è un amore reciproco.
Il loro amore va avanti molto bene.
Il loro amore, invece, sta andando a rovescio.

d.
Lui ha sempre grande fortuna.
La mia fortuna, invece, è piccola.
La loro fortuna è più ampia di quello che credono.
Anche la fortuna dei tuoi cugini è vasta.

12. Give potential source domains for delivering the following concepts, providing one or two examples for each:

Example: l'amore
[sapore]
Il mio amore è *dolce.*
Il loro amore è diventato *amaro.*

speranza
giustizia
amicizia

tempo
sapienza
amore
idee

13. Explain the difference among metaphor, metonymy, and irony.

8
Discourse

....

You can stroke people with words.

F. Scott Fitzgerald (1896–1940)

In previous chapters we have been taking a close look at the internal workings of the Italian language through the microscope of linguistics, highlighting procedures that linguists typically use to examine how the bits and pieces cohere to produce a language. This type of analysis is akin to the chemist's investigation of the structure of molecules, of the kinds of molecular structures that are possible, and of how these constituents make up larger structures such as organs.

However, the linguistic analysis of Italian would not be complete if we stopped at this point, for an appreciation of the structure of the language is not an end in itself – like the appreciation of an abstract painting. Like an organism, language is a highly adaptive and context-sensitive instrument that is shaped by forces largely external to it. The phonological, morphological, syntactic, and semantic levels are not only interrelated structurally, but are also highly susceptible to the subtle influences of the discourse situation to which they are applied in tandem. The internal structures of language are pliable entities that are responsive to social situations. *Langue* and *parole* are really two sides of the same coin, rather than separate dimensions.

Consider the following common scenario in which a 17-year-old high-school student is saying good-bye, first to his English teacher, second to his mother, and third to a peer:

Good-bye to English teacher:	Good-bye, sir!
Good-bye to mother:	See ya later, ma!
Good-bye to a peer:	I gotta split, man!

Clearly, these are not interchangeable utterances – the adolescent would not say 'I gotta split, man!' to a teacher or 'Good-bye, sir!' to a peer. This simple, yet instructive example shows that the choice of language forms and the types of structural patterns that are utilized in specific situations will vary predictably. This kind of practical knowledge is clearly different from the knowledge of structural relations in themselves. It constitutes a pragmatic form of knowledge known as **communicative competence**.

Corresponding utterances for saying good-bye in Italian are, with some variation, as follows:

Good-bye to Italian teacher:	ArrivederLa, professore!
Good-bye to mother:	Ci vediamo più tardi, ma!
Good-bye to a peer:	A-oh! fatti vivo!

The study of discourse competence falls under the rubric of **pragmatics**, the branch of linguistics that deals with those aspects of form and meaning that vary according to situational and social variables. It deals with *who* says *what* to *whom* in specific situations. In short, it studies the patterns that govern the appropriate use of language in social contexts.

Speech Acts

In Chapter 2, and again briefly in Chapter 7, we discussed the notion of **speech act**, one of the central concepts in discourse analysis. A speech act is an utterance that aims to achieve some effect. The utterance *Sta' attento!* for instance, would have the same effect as putting a hand in front of someone to block him from, say, crossing the road carelessly. A judge's statement *La condanno all'ergastolo* ('I sentence you to life imprisonment') has the same effect as if the judge had marched the accused to prison and locked him up. In effect, a speech act is a replacement for some action.

There are various versions of speech act theory. The central idea in all of these is to identify the speech acts that are dictated by the situation, along with the linguistic resources that these subsume. Speech acts allow people to carry out such social functions as:

- initiating contact
- ending contact
- thanking

- congratulating
- showing satisfaction
- approving
- disapproving
- showing surprise
- offering to do something
- renouncing
- suggesting
- warning
- begging
- exchanging facts
- reporting
- comparing
- narrating
- asking for opinions
- remembering
- forgetting
- keeping track of time
- expressing spatial relations
- expressing notions of entity
- expressing notions of quantity
- self-portrayal
- explicating family relations
- explicating social relations
- understanding
- getting angry
- arguing
- reacting to statements
- ordering
- demanding

Although there is much leeway in the linguistic choices that can be made to match a function, the choices are not completely open to personal whims. Indeed, speech act theory argues strongly that language is well suited to matching each situation with appropriate categories, and that the number of categories is constrained by cultural and historical factors.

One line of research in speech act theory suggests that many situations are so typical that the speech forms used for them are highly formulaic. This kind of knowledge is thought to be stored in memory in the form of **frames**, which are adapted to fit with present reality and altered as required. For example, ordering from a menu at a restaurant constitutes a frame in which both waiter and customer enter into a kind of dialogue that seems to flow in a script-like fashion. Here is a sample of the various options that the first few parts of the 'ordering script' would include:

Waiter:	Cosa prende?
	Prego?
	Mi dica
Customer:	Per cominciare, un antipasto
	Com'è l'antipasto stasera?
etc.	

Completing the script will be assigned as an exercise below. Such frames exist in many areas of social discourse: for example, asking for services (at a bank, at a post office), negotiating a transaction at a gas station, at a store, and so on.

Conversational Devices

Conversations of all kinds are constructed with *devices* that are intended to maintain the smooth flow of communication. Consider, for instance, the following two texts, which tell the same story in different ways:

1. *Maria è andata al negozio ieri. Maria ha incontrato un'amica al negozio. Maria e l'amica si sono salutate. Era molto tempo che Maria non vedeva l'amica.*
2. *Maria è andata al negozio ieri. Lì ci ha incontrato un'amica. Le due si sono salutate. Era molto tempo che non si vedevano.*

The first story sounds stilted and odd, even though each sentence is well formed. The second version reads more like ordinary conversation because in Italian, as in other languages, repetition is discouraged in normal style. For this reason, the language makes available several devices that allow for the same information to be carried without the repetition.

Devices that refer back to some word or syntactic category are called **anaphoric**. In (2) above, *ci* refers back to *il negozio*, *le due* to *Maria e un'amica*. The opposite of an anaphoric device is a **cataphoric** device – that is, a word or particle that anticipates some other word. For example, in the sentence *Anche se lui te lo negherà, ti giuro che Marco l'ha fatto,* the pronoun *lui* refers ahead to *Marco.* Subject and object pronouns, locative particles, demonstratives, adverbs, for instance, often function as anaphoric and cataphoric particles in conversations and narrative texts.

There are many other kinds of such devices in conversation (note the use of the reciprocal tense *si vedevano* to replace *Maria non vedeva l'amica*). Their function is to keep the conversation flowing smoothly without undue reiteration. This shows once again the intrinsic interconnection between discourse and the language system. Indeed, in a discourse model of language, once would classify such categories as pronouns and locative particles as conversational devices above all else, and then explain their *raison d'être* as communicative rather than purely grammatical. These devices link together sentences in a cohesive fashion.

Another common conversational device is known as a gambit. A **gambit** is a word or phrase used to open a conversation, to keep it going, to make it smooth. In English, for example, the following are gambits with three different functions:

1. uh huh ...ya ... hmm ... aha ...
2. You agree with me, don't you?
3. May I ask you a question?

The grunt-like expressions uttered in (1) constitute a strategy for acknowledging that one is listening to an interlocutor, especially on the phone. Total silence is not an appropriate gambit in English, although it is in other languages. In Italian a different gambit is deployed in this case, namely a series of words such as *sì ... capisco ... eh già ... vero ...*

The question in (2) is called a *tag question*, a question added on at the end of the sentence that is designed to seek approval, agreement, consent, and so forth. The same device is found in Italian. The following are examples of Italian tags:

1. Ho ragione, non credi?
2. Sei d'accordo, non è vero?
3. Ti piace, no?

Utterance (3) is an opening gambit – that is, a strategy for starting a conversation, for taking a turn in a conversation, or for entering into a conversation. In Italian, expressions such as *Posso? Chiedo scusa, ma potrebbe dirmi ...?* and *Permesso?* are all opening gambits.

Another type of conversational device is known as a **repair**. When there is a minor breakdown in a conversation, or something is not explained properly, then repairs allow the speaker to solve the problem. The word *Scusa*, for example, is such a device: *È arrivato lunedì. Scusa, volevo dire martedì.*

Nonverbal Communication

Face-to-face conversations invariably involve the simultaneous deployment of nonverbal modes of communication (facial expressions, posturing, and gesturing of some kind) that accompany the vocal utterance. These may seem to be disconnected to the language used, but a closer analysis reveals that the two are highly interconnected. Consider the use of hand **gestures** during conversation.

Although there are cross-cultural similarities in gesture, substantial differences exist both in the extent to which gesture is used and in the interpretations given to its particular uses. For example, the head gestures for *yes* and *no* used in the Balkans seem inverted to other Europeans. In 1979, the anthropologist Desmond Morris, together with several of his associates at Oxford University, examined twenty gestures in forty different areas of Europe, publishing the results in a widely quoted book titled *Gestures: Their Origins and Distributions*. The research team found some rather fascinating things. For instance, they discovered that many of the gestures had several meanings, depending on culture: for example, a tap on the side of the head can indicate 'stupidity' or 'intelligence,' depending on the cultural context. Morris also found that most of the gestural signifiers were used in many countries.

Many linguists consider gesture to be a more fundamental form of communication than vocal language. A pragmatic, anecdotal 'confirmation' of this viewpoint can be obtained when you are travelling in a country whose language you do not speak. In order to communicate with the people on the street, in a hotel, in a store, and so on, one instinctively resorts to gesture in order to get a message across or to negotiate meaning. For example, if one were to describe an automobile to someone by means of gesture, one would instinctively use the hands to portray a steering wheel and the motion used to steer a car, accompanying this gesture, perhaps, with an imitative sound of a motor. This anecdotal scenario suggests that gesture is a fundamental mode of communication.

Gesture can, and often does, replace vocal language for carrying out interactional protocols such as greeting, affirming, and negating, as well as for communicating obscenities. Italians, in fact, are famous for being able to 'carry out a conversation' almost exclusively through gesture.

The most suggestive evidence that gesture may perhaps have been the evolutionary antecedent of vocal language is the fact that it is a universal mode of representation that can satisfy all basic communicative needs. The developmental literature has documented, moreover, that children invariably pass through an initial stage of pointing and gesturing before they develop vocal language. It is intriguing to note that, although vocal language eventually becomes the dominant form of communication, the gestural modality does not vanish completely. It remains a functional subsystem of vocal language that can always be utilized as a more generic form of communication when an interaction is otherwise impossible. This happens typically, as mentioned above, when two interlocutors speak different languages. And, of course, in individuals with impaired vocal organs, gesture constitutes the primary mode of communication (in addition to writing).

Some fascinating research by the linguist David McNeill shows, moreover, how gesture is interconnected with discourse. McNeill videotaped a large sample of people as they spoke, gathering a vast amount of data on the kinds of gestures that typically accompany speech. McNeill's findings suggest that gestures are complementary components of vocal communication, allowing the speaker to exhibit images that cannot be shown overtly in speech, as well as images of what the speaker is thinking about. Speech and gesture constitute a single, integrated communication system in which both cooperate to express the person's meanings.

On the basis of his findings, McNeill was able to classify gestures into five main categories. First, there are **iconic gestures**, which, as their name suggests, bear a close resemblance to the referent of an utterance: for example, when describing a scene from a story in which a character bends a tree back to the ground, a speaker observed by McNeill appeared to grip something and pull it back. His gesture was, in effect, a visual representation of the action talked about, revealing both his memory image and his point of view (since he could have taken the part of the character or the tree instead).

Second, **metaphoric gestures** are also pictorial, but their content is abstract. For example, McNeill observed a male speaker announcing that what he had just seen was a cartoon, simultaneously raising up his hands as if offering his listener a kind of object. He was obviously not referring to the cartoon itself, but to the 'genre' of the cartoon. His gesture created and displayed this genre as if it were an object, placing it into an act of offering to the listener. This type of gesture typically accompanies utterances that contain expressions such as *presenting an idea, putting forth an idea, offering advice*, and so on.

Third, **beat gestures** resemble the beating of a musical tempo. The speaker's hand moves along with the rhythmic pulsation of speech, in the form of a simple flick of the hand or fingers up and down, or back and forth. Beats are used to mark the introduction of new characters, summarize the action, or introduce new themes during the utterance.

Fourth, are **cohesive gestures**. These serve to show how separate parts of an utterance are supposed to hold together. Beats emphasize sequentiality, cohesives globality. Cohesives can take iconic, metaphoric, or beat form. They unfold through a repetition of the same gesture form, movement, or location in the gesture space. It is the repetition that is meant to convey cohesiveness.

Finally, **deictic gestures** are aimed not at an existing physical place, but at an abstract concept that had occurred earlier in the conversation. They reveal that we perceive concepts as having a physical location in space. Some deictic pointing gestures are really counterparts to spatial, temporal, and personal deictic forms:

su	=	finger points in an upward direction
giù	=	finger points in a downward direction
io	=	finger points to oneself
tu	=	finger points to a person
etc.		

McNeill's work gives us a good idea of how the gestural mode of representation intersects with the vocal one in normal discourse. It would seem to be the case that accompanying gestures reveal an inner need to support what one is saying orally. This would explain why, for instance, someone sitting on a beach can hardly resist drawing with the fingers on the smooth surface of the sand as a means of clarifying what he or she is talking about.

A Model of Discourse

So far we have been looking at such things as speech acts, conversational devices, and gestures. However, we have not incorporated these into a model of verbal communication. Among the various models put forward over the years, the one by the Moscow-born linguist and semiotician Roman Jakobson, who carried out most of his work in the United States, is perhaps the most insightful one. Jakobson posited six 'constituents' that characterize all speech acts:

1. an **addresser** who initiates a communication;
2. a **message** that she or he recognizes must refer to something other than itself;
3. an **addressee** who is the intended receiver of the message;
4. a **context** that permits the addressee to recognize that the message is referring to something other than itself: for example, if someone were crying out '*Aiuto*,' lying motionless on the ground, then one would easily understand that the message is referring to a concrete situation;
5. a mode of **contact** by which a message is delivered (the physical channel) and the primary social and psychological connections that are established between the addresser and addressee;
6. a **code** providing the signs and structural patterns for constructing and deciphering messages.

Jakobson then pointed out that each of these constituents determines a different communicative function:

1. **emotive** = the presence of the addresser's emotions, attitudes, social status, etc. in the message;
2. **conative** = the intended effect – physical, psychological, social, etc. – that the message is expected to have on the addressee;

3. **referential** = a message constructed to convey information (*Via Nazionale si trova a due isolati da qui*);
4. **poetic** = a message constructed to deliver meanings effectively, like poetry (as in advertising);
5. **phatic** = a message designed to establish social contact (*Ciao, come va?*);
6. **metalingual** = a message designed to refer to the code used (*La parola nome è un nome*).

Jakobson's analysis of verbal communication suggests that discourse goes well beyond a situation of simple information transfer – it is motivated and shaped by the setting, the message contents, the code(s), the participants, and the goals of each interlocutor. Discourse makes an emotional claim on everyone in the social situation. It is a form of acting, of presenting self through language. Communicators must know how to start and end the conversation, how to make themselves understood, how to respond to their partner's statements, how to be sensitive to the concerns of others, how to take turns, and how to listen.

Jakobson's model raises the larger question of what is communication. Verbal communication between two people is not a simple transfer of signals. It is an outgrowth of interaction based on various modes of expression – gestures, the vocal language, the necessity to engage in joint action, and so on – that have all played a part in bringing about communicative competence. Humans are not the only creatures that communicate. All animals exchange signals that help them find food, migrate, or reproduce. However, while other animals use a limited range of signals to communicate needs, humans have developed complex systems that transcend a simple deployment to satisfy physical needs. Indeed, humans talk not only to procure food or to satisfy urges, but also to express ideas and emotions, to tell stories and remember the past, and to portray imaginary worlds.

Since at least the mid-1950s, some linguists and anthropologists have turned their attention to testing out the possibility of teaching human language to animals. There is no doubt that animals and humans exchange signals and thus communicate at a rudimentary level. Tones of voice, postures, movements are the signifying elements of an 'interspecies communication code.' This code taps basic sensory structures that cut across human and animal communication systems, emerging 'adaptively' from our shared sensory experiences.

However, language is something that seems to be unique to the human species. Although the animals in the experiments have shown the capacity to learn vocabulary and elementary syntax, there is no evidence that they can decipher the meaning of a simple metaphorical statement like *The professor is a snake*, or of a statement such as *The house is in session now*. The message inherent in such human forms can be received successfully by another organism only if that organism has access to the same kinds of cognitive and emotional structures that undergird human message making. It is unlikely that these are present in other species.

Narrative and Discourse

A **narrative** is a *text* that is constructed to describe in sequence a perceived causal and interconnected sequence of events involving characters in time and space. The narrative may be purely fact-based, as in a newspaper report or a psychoanalytic session, or fictional, as in a novel, comic strip, film, for instance. Needless to say, it is often difficult, if not impossible, to determine the boundary line between narrative fact and fiction. Indeed, even in talking about oneself, fiction is often intermingled with fact in order to give the portrayal more logical consistency. This is called the 'Othello effect' by psychologists. It is a kind of lying in order to emphasize the truth.

The serious study of narrative structure was initiated after the scholar Vladimir Propp argued in the late 1920s that ordinary discourse was built on this structure. According to Propp, a relatively small number of universal 'narrative units,' or plot themes, go into the make-up of a 'plot grammar.' This would explain why narrative is the medium through which children learn about the world. Stories of imaginary beings and events allow children to make sense of the real world, providing the intelligible formats that mobilize the child's natural ability to learn from context. Psychological research has shown that narrative discourse underlies how children come to understand themselves and the social world in which they live. Narrative brings the developing human organism into the arena of culture. It is the form of discourse that gives pattern and continuity to their early perceptions and experiences. Children respond to plot, character, and setting without training. They instinctively understand any representation that links events in a narrative way. By age four or five, children are able to manage and negotiate narratives by themselves, especially during play, when they create imaginary stories designed to give others watching them a framework for interpreting their actions.

Follow-Up Activities

1. Define the following terms and notions in your own words:

   discourse
   communicative competence
   pragmatics
   speech act
   frame
   anaphoric device
   cataphoric device
   gambit
   repair
   gesture
   iconic gesture
   metaphoric gesture
   beat gesture
   cohesive gesture
   deictic gesture
   addresser
   message
   addressee
   context
   contact
   code
   emotive function
   conative function
   referential function
   poetic function
   phatic function
   metalingual function
   narrative

2. How would a 17-year-old say hello to the following (in Italian)?

a peer
a teacher
his or her mother or father

3. What effect would the following utterances have?

   Example: Vieni qui!
   (This has the same effect of grabbing someone and directing him
   or her towards oneself.)

   Sta' zitto!
   Aspettami qui!
   Dove vai?
   Chi è quella persona?
   Ciao, Alessandro.
   Ecco Laura e Marcello.
   Ciao a tutti!

4. Provide a frame (or script) for carrying out the following situational functions.

   Example: Ordering a meal at a restaurant
   Possible frame:
   Cameriere: Cosa prende?
   Cliente: Per primo, un piatto di spaghetti alla carbonara.
   Cameriere: Per secondo?
   etc.

   Asking a policeman directions to find a street
   Answering the phone
   Making an appointment with a doctor
   Asking a bank teller to make a deposit

5. Identify the function(s) of each utterance.

   Example: Mi chiamo Sandra Mazzetti.
   (Introducing/presenting oneself)

   Ciao, Claudia. Come va?
   Ho mal di testa.

Pazienza!
A domani!
Come sta?
Buongiorno.
Buonasera.
Buonanotte.
Come stai?
Alessandro, ti piace l'Aida?
Non mi piace l'opera.

6. Rewrite the following passage using appropriate anaphoric, cataphoric, and other kinds of conversational devices that would render it more cohesive and stylistically appropriate.

   *Alessandro ama Giulia. Ieri Alessandro ha visto Giulia, mentre
   Giulia camminava lungo la strada. Alessandro conosce Giulia da
   quattro anni, e adesso Alessandro è innamorato di Giulia. Alessandro ha chiamato Giulia, e poi Alessandro ha dato a Giulia un
   bacio. Alessandro ha dato a Giulia un bacio perchè Alessandro
   ama Giulia. Ma Giulia non ama Alessandro, allora Giulia non ha
   apprezzato quel suo bacio.*

7. Underline and identify the anaphoric and cataphoric devices in
   each of the following.

   Example: Prima che lui <u>la</u> chiamasse, Giulia sapeva già tutto.
   la is a cataphoric pronoun (anticipating *Giulia).*

   A Marisa piace il compact disc che le ho dato ieri.
   Gli ho dato tutto, a Corrado.
   Chi ha mangiato la pizza? L'ho mangiata io.
   Quando sei andato a Venezia? Ci sono andato due anni fa.
   Quando sei tornato da Venezia? Ne sono tornato quattro mesi fa.
   Ne vuoi di carne?

8. Identify the type of gambit used in the following utterances, along
   with its function.

   Example: Vieni anche tu, spero?
   spero = tag question gambit beseeching the person to come

Capisco ... capisco ... sì ... sì
Non ci credo, e tu?
Sei d'accordo, no?
Se mi permetti, vorrei ...

9. Describe the function(s) of gesture in conversation.

10. What kinds of gestures would you use to convey the following meanings?

stop
get up
greeting someone
taking leave of someone
anger
happiness
confusion
agreement
affirmation
negation

11. Do you think that gesture is more primitive than vocal language? If so, provide reasons.

12. Summarize David McNeill's findings on the use of gesture during conversation.

13. Give examples of the following types of gestures:

iconic
metaphoric
beat
cohesive
deictic

14. Describe Jakobson's model of communication.

15. Using Jakobson's model, take any lifestyle ad from an Italian magazine and then identify which constituents and functions apply to the decipherment of the ad.

16. What functions does communication serve?

17. Explain the interconnection between narrative and discourse.

9
Variation

All things change, nothing is extinguished.

Ovid (43 BC–AD 17)

In the opening chapter, we briefly discussed dialectal variation in Italy. The topic of variation is an important one in linguistics. In addition to regional dialectal variation, languages vary along a social continuum. As we saw in the previous chapter, social situations are central in motivating the use of different forms in specific circumstances. For example, in certain dialects of American English, the pronunciation of the *r* sound has been linked to social class. In expressions such as *fourth floor*, some people pronounce the /r/ and others do not, and the usage of the phoneme is claimed to be consistent within a given socioeconomic niche. According to one study of English as used in New York City, people aspiring to move from the lower middle class to the upper middle class attach prestige to pronouncing the /r/. Sometimes they even overcorrect their speech to pronounce /r/ where those they emulate may not.

As we saw in the opening chapter, in Italy, the crux of the *questione della lingua* has always centred around what the ideal speech is for all Italians, that is, which version of the vernacular is the one to emulate. The linguistic unification of Italy around the Tuscan literary standard is only a few decades old. Before that, different dialects were spoken in homes and communities throughout Italy, each reflecting its own rich cultural history, and each with its own situation-sensitive functions. Many of these unfortunately are disappearing in a world susceptible to the 'levelling effect' of electronic media. But variation has not disappeared. As in all languages, diversity and variability are built into the use of Italian as the result of geographical and social factors.

Regional Variation

As discussed in the opening chapter, the Italian dialects are all sister languages, descendants of the same mother tongue, Latin. During the Middle Ages, the dialects prospered. But over the centuries the expansion of dialectal use was checked, in part, by the rise of Tuscany as a political and cultural force.

To this day, however, many Italians are attached to their local dialectal speech. Even the inevitable push for assimilation into the linguistic mainstream, which gained unswerving momentum in the middle part of the twentieth century, has not completely severed the crucial verbal links that many Italians maintain to their dialectal past. People across the peninsula continue to display a profound sense of pride in their dialect backgrounds.

Speaking a dialect leaves traces, first and foremost, on how the standard language is pronounced. Recall, from the first chapter, that northern Italian dialects were characterized by the phenomenon of simplification, whereby double consonants are simplified to single ones: /C:/ > /C/. Thus, logically, speakers from those regions tend to pronounce double consonants as single ones:

/karamel:a/ > /karamela/ (*caramella*)
/trop:o/ > /tropo/ (*troppo*)
/fer:o/ > /fero/ (*ferro*)

In the Neapolitan dialect, the /s/ is palatalized before nondental consonants: /s/ > /ʃ/. This trait is carried over, by many speakers, to the pronunciation of Italian: /spero/ > /ʃpero/ (*spero*). Pronunciation habits such as these are disappearing more and more, but they still persist in many areas of Italy, especially in the case of older speakers.

Regionally based variation is not limited to pronunciation. In northern Italy there is a tendency to use the present perfect to describe virtually all past actions (e.g., *Sono andato al cinema la settimana scorsa*); in many parts of southern Italy, especially in Sicily, the tendency instead is to use the past absolute (*Andai al cinema la settimana scorsa*). Referring to a watermelon as *cocomero, anguria,* or *melone* also falls along dialectal lines as well: *cocomero* is used primarily in the central and south-central parts of Italy, *anguria* in northern Italy, and *melone* in many parts of southern Italy.

The list of regional traits could go on and on. Suffice it to say that such variation is an intrinsic part of the Italian situation, even in an age of media-induced linguistic levelling. It will be interesting to see what role computer-based communication (e-mail, Internet, etc.) will have on further entrenching the tendency towards levelling.

Variation Outside Italy

The use of Italian and its dialects in immigrant communities, such as those that formed in North America after World War II, also presents instances of variation that, in microcosm, mirror the peninsular situation. In such communities, for first- and even second-generation speakers, the local dialect constituted the code with which they carried out communication within the family and within communities of same-dialect speakers. A common Italian code for communication among speakers of different dialects also emerged. This 'common vernacular' has been called, colloquially, *Italiese*, a blend of *italiano* and *inglese*.

Italiese is so called because it contains a large number of words borrowed from English to refer to everyday items and notions. As pointed out in the opening chapter, the words taken from English are known as loanwords. Recall, moreover, that loanwords are normally nativized in predictable ways. Thus, for example, borrowed nouns are assigned a gender through the addition of final vowels:

garbage	→	*garbiccio*
mortgage	→	*morgheggio*
switch	→	*suiccia*
fence	→	*fenza*
etc.		

Within Italiese, as within the Italian spoken on the peninsula, there is predictable regional variation: the actual pronunciation of the loanwords will vary according to the speaker's original dialect of origin (northern speakers, for instance, would pronounce a word like *suiccia* with a single consonant).

In addition to loanwords, Italiese is replete with calques. **Calques** are syntactic strings that have been translated literally:

| downtown | → | *bassa città* |
| it looks good | → | *guarda bene* |

to make a call → *fare il telefono*
etc.

In the domain of morphological nativization, the salient feature of Italiese is its regularity. For instance, all verb loanwords are nativized to the first conjugation – the most regular and the most frequent one in the Italian verb system:

to push   → *pusciare*
to smash   → *smesciare*
to squeeze   → *squisare*
etc.

The primary reason why loanwords and calques are so plentiful in Italiese is need. The borrowings that underwent nativization were, in fact, those that the immigrants required in order to refer to the objects and ideas in their new physical and social environment. Lacking an appropriate dialectal word for *mortgage*, for instance, immigrants were forced to adopt the English word and make it their own linguistically.

Such 'hybrid languages' are found in all areas of the world where a dominant language is in contact with a nondominant one. Known as *contact phenomena*, the features that the nondominant language accepts are usually those that are so frequent in social context that they surreptitiously make their way into its various linguistic levels, or else they are those features that speakers need to carry out appropriate conversations in context.

Some have referred to Italiese as a *pidgin*, but this is not correct. The Italian spoken in North America is not a simplified version of peninsular Italian; it is simply an 'external' dialect of the language. A **pidgin**, on the other hand, is an auxiliary language (a language used for communication by groups that have different native tongues) that develops when people speaking different languages are brought together and forced to develop a common means of communication without sufficient time to learn each other's native language properly. Typically, a pidgin language derives most of its lexicon from one of the languages. Its morphological and syntactic structure, however, either will be highly variable, reflecting the structures of each speaker's native language, or may in time become stabilized in a manner different from the morphological and syntactic patterns of the language that contributed most of its vocabulary.

A **creole** language arises in a contact situation similar to that which produced Italiese. But even this designation for Italiese would be incorrect. Creoles, like Italiese, take most of their vocabulary from a single dominant language. But Italiese is different from a creole in that it retains its indigenous Italian phonological and grammatical structure intact. A creole, on the other hand, is highly susceptible to phonological and morphological influences from the dominant language.

Social Varieties

Social varieties of a language, called *social dialects*, or **sociolects**, are versions shaped by social factors. Sociolects often develop due to social divisions within a society, such as those of socioeconomic class and religion. For example, in England, the pronunciation of /h/, as in *hat*, conveys social information. Members of certain social groups often adopt a particular pronunciation of /h/ as a way of distinguishing themselves from other social groups. Similarly, the inhabitants of Martha's Vineyard, in Massachusetts, have adopted particular vowel pronunciations to distinguish themselves from people vacationing on the island.

Slang, argot, and jargon are more specialized terms for certain sociolects usually defined by their specialized vocabularies. **Slang** refers to the coinage and use of informal vocabulary, especially short-lived coinages, that do not belong to a language's standard vocabulary. **Argot** refers to the coinage and use of a nonstandard vocabulary by secret groups, particularly criminal organizations, usually intended to render utterances incomprehensible to outsiders. **Jargon** refers to the specialized use of a vocabulary by those in a particular trade or profession (e.g., legal jargon, scientific jargon, academic jargon).

In Italian, as in other languages, socially induced variation is a fact of life. It is impossible here to give an in-depth treatment of the many sociolects that are shaped by such variables as age, gender, class, and occupation. So, for the sake of brevity, we will focus on the slang spoken by Italian teenagers.

Young people have always resorted to code words in order to strengthen group identity and to set themselves apart from others. Medieval university students, for instance, used the word *lupi* (wolves) to refer to spies who reported other students for using the vernacular instead of Latin. If adolescent slang, as it is commonly called, has a specific social function, then it can hardly be considered a form of aberrant communicative behaviour. For this reason, it has alternatively been called *pubilect*, a contraction of *puberty* and *dialect*.* **Pubilect** can be defined simply as the sociolect of teenagers. It is a code through which teenagers signal the important differences they see between themselves and older people and a primary vehicle for carrying out appropriate social interaction with peers.

The whole gamut of emotional responses that teenagers have to their immediate context, as well as the creative strategies they employ to handle specific social situations, are reflected in the ways in which they program their discourse efforts. The main categories of adolescent discourse programming are: emotive language programming, connotative language programming, and clique-coded language programming.

Emotive Language Programming

The term *emotive*, as we saw in the previous chapter, was used by Roman Jakobson to refer to the fact that a speaker's emotions, attitudes, and social status shape the specific ways in which she or he will construct verbal messages in particular social contexts. Emotivity varies according to type of message. *Emotive language programming (ELP)* manifests itself, for instance, in intensified language markers, increased rates of speech delivery, overwrought intonation contours, and highly emotional voice modulations. For instance, current North American pubilect utterances such as 'He's sooooo cute!' 'She's faaaaar out!' and 'That's amaaaazing!' exemplify the common emotive pattern of overstressing words by a prolongation of the tonic vowel. This feature surfaces in Italian pubilect as well: *'Che beeeello!' 'Stupeeeendoooo!' 'Ma coooome?' 'Hei, ma sei un macaaaaco, eh?'* and so on.

In North American adolescent talk, utterances such as 'We called her up (?) (intonation contour like a question) ... but she wasn't there (?) (same contour)... so we hung up (?) (same contour)' show a pattern of rising contours (as if each sentence were interrogative). Called colloquially by the media as 'uptalk,' this feature is, in effect, an implicit tag questioning strategy. A *tag*, as we saw in the previous chapter, is a word, phrase, or clause added by an addresser to a sentence to emphasize his or her point, to seek the approval of the listener, or to ascertain

---

* See M. Danesi, *Cool: The Signs and Meanings of Adolescence* (Toronto: University of Toronto Press, 1994).

some reaction: 'She's coming tomorrow, *isn't she?*' 'That was a good course, *right?*' etc. The 'uptalk' pattern demonstrated by adolescents is, in effect, a tag question without the tag. This common ELP trait probably indicates the need of teenagers to ensure the full participation of their interlocutors in their discourse.

In Italy this feature surfaces in two main ways: (1) it shows up as an *eh* tag – *'Allora ti piace, eh?'* *'No, no, eh, non è mica vero, eh?'*; (2) it surfaces as a kind of hesitation groan, '*mmmmm,*' that is interjected throughout the sentence – *'Devo, mmmmm, dire che, mmmmm, non capisco, mmmmm,'* *'Io, mmmmm, penso, che quello là, mmmmm, è un cretino,'* and so forth.

Another manifestation of emotivity in Italian pubilect is the overuse of: (1) interjections and exclamations – *'Hei, cosa succede?'* *'Boh, e chi ci capisce niente?'* *'Ah-oh, ma che cacchio fai?'*; (2) swear words – *'Hei, cazzone, che fai?'* *'Sei proprio un leccamerda'*; and (3) *cioè,* which is the Italian equivalent of *like* ('*Like,* I called him up, but, *like,* he wasn't sure, if he, *like,* could come ...') – *'L'ho chiamato, cioè, a casa, cioè, quando non c'era lei, cioè.'*

Essentially, all these manifestations of ELP reveal a strong tendency in adolescents to project their feelings and to seek approval of what they are saying. There is nothing particularly surprising about this function of pubilect. Adult speech can also be highly emotive. Adults commonly lengthen sounds for emphasis and regularly use intonation patterns to express emotional states, to emphasize something, or to shock someone. The difference between ELP in adult and adolescent speech lies in the degree and extent to which it characterizes the programming of discourse.

Connotative Language Programming

Connotative language programming (CLP) refers to the tendency of adolescents to coin descriptive words, or to extend the meaning of existing words, in highly connotative ways. Connotation is at the core of the adolescent's linguistic modelling of reality. In the mid-1980s words such as *loser, gross out, air-head, slime-bucket,* and others were in widespread use in North American pubilect. More recently, *vomatose, thicko, burger-brain,* and *knob,* have gained currency. But no matter from what generation of teens the words come, the programming mechanism is the same – it is grounded in a constant need to describe others and meaningful social situations in highly connotative ways.

The CLP category is a highly productive one in Italian pubilect as well: for example, a *togo* is someone who is defined as 'bello, stupendo, divertente' (= English *cool*); a *grasta* is a female teen who is 'cretina, stupida, scema' (= English *loser*); and a *secchione* is someone who is 'troppo studioso' (= English *dork* or *nerd*). Other CLP expressions coined in the 1990s are as follows

- *'Camomillati!'* (= Cool it!)
- 'Perché *ti buchi* sempre?' (= Why do you always shoot up?)
- 'Devo *andare in catalessi* presto' (= I have to get some sleep soon)
- 'lo *scocciofono*' (= the telephone)
- 'lo *stregone*' (= the doctor)
- 'Andiamo col tuo *ferro*, eh?' (= Shall we go with your car?)
- 'Dammi un po' di *ossigeno*' (= Give me a cigarette)
- 'Loro si *francobollano* spesso' (= They kiss a lot)
- 'Ci vai mai a *scimmiare*?' (= Do you ever go dancing?)
- 'la *caverna*' (= the home)
- 'Sono *asfaltato*' (= I'm broke)
- *'fior di fragola*' (= beautiful female)
- 'il *museo*' (= school)
- *'Fantasmati!'* (= Get out of here!)
- 'gli *spinelli*' (= cigarettes)

Research on pubilects throughout the world shows that such terms have a very short lifespan. By comparison with vocabulary change in the language as a whole, which sometimes takes centuries, the rate of change in teen vocabularies is greatly accelerated. However, the same research also shows that, recently, many of these terms are gaining general currency, cutting across regional and dialectal boundaries.

Psychologically, CLP reveals rather conspicuously that adolescents are keenly sensitive to bodily appearance and image, as well as to the perceived sociability of peers. At puberty the changes in physical appearance, and the emotional changes that accompany them, are perceived as overwhelming. Consequently, teenagers become inordinately concerned about their own appearance and behaviour, believing that everyone is constantly observing them. To offset this preoccupation with self-image, they talk about how others act, behave, and appear.

Language is thus used as an evaluative grid for assessing peer appearance and sociability, thus deflecting attention away from the self.

Clique-Coded Language Programming

Teenagers speak primarily about the themes and topics that are of direct interest to the specific cliques to which they belong. *Clique-coded language programming (CCLP)*, therefore, refers to this feature of pubilect. Clique membership entails knowing what to say, and how to say it, in appropriate contexts. Teenagers achieve relative status in the fluctuating hierarchy of their clique by learning how to advantageously manipulate their verbal interactions with peers. Teens in some cliques will typically use swear words to assert a position of dominance, to attract and maintain an audience, and to assert themselves when other speakers have the floor. Those with ineffectual verbal skills will either become clique outcasts or be compelled to accept lower status within the clique hierarchy.

The goal during group ritual verbal exchanges is to 'keep one's cool' by not letting the opponent realize that one is wavering. The ability to respond to even personal insults in a nonserious manner is a critical skill needed for successful participation in ritual insulting. Verbal conflict skills are developed through frequent participation in duelling matches. It is for this reason that those individuals who hang out more with the group seem to get a firmer command of the techniques needed to succeed at verbal duelling. The peer audience participating in this activity acts as a kind of critical audience. If the exchange ends with someone verbally destroying the other, the audience will invariably proceed to ridicule and defame the loser. In many cases, this post-defeat mockery unfolds in terms of a stage-like scornful scenario.

The themes that surface most frequently in clique exchanges are centred around peer-related themes and events – for example, music preferences, sexuality, automobile ownership, physical appearance, inter- and intra-clique relations. Especially prominent is reference to the panorama of daily events associated with school life. The high school is where friendships are forged, clique allegiances established, conflictual behaviours between teens and cliques developed, clique identities manufactured, and so on. The school is perceived by many adolescents more as a social system than a learning institution. Newcomers must pass initiation rites; outsiders are looked upon with suspicion and must be introduced into the school by a school member; *losers* are marginalized.

Aspects of Linguistic Change

In the opening chapter, we painted a schematic historical picture of the origins and evolution of Italian and its dialects. The approach to the study of language focused on describing diachronically based variation. In this final section, we come, full circle, back to this topic. This time our emphasis will be on tying together the loose theoretical ends we left in the opening chapter: we will discuss the reasons for, and the processes that underlie, change in languages.

Languages continually undergo changes, although speakers of a language are usually unaware of the changes as they are occurring. For instance, American English has experienced an ongoing change in which the phonemic difference between the words *cot* and *caught* is being lost. The changes become more dramatic after longer periods of time. Modern Italian readers may require notes to understand fully the writings of Dante, and even of Leopardi. The Italian of the fourteenth century differs enough from the modern language that many readers nowadays prefer a translation into modern Italian. Indeed, many of the great works of Italian literature and philosophy are being 'updated' linguistically for use in high schools throughout Italy.

Sound Change

Historical change can affect all components of language. Sound change is the area of language change that has received the most attention by linguists. One of the major sound changes in the history of the Italian language, as we have seen, concerns the vowels. Recall that Latin had five basic vowels, with each one being pronounced long or short. The opposition /V/ ~ /V:/ was phonemic: for example, /o:s/ ~ /os/ = *mouth* ~ *bone*. This phonemic distinction was lost in the Romance languages, even if its vestiges have remained in the form of a complementary distribution rule that we called *complementary lengthening* in Chapter 4.

Various theories and explanations have been put forward to explain such changes. Perhaps the most widely accepted one was put forward in the 1950s by the French linguist André Martinet, who claimed that languages change in the direction of least effort. Calling it the principle of 'economic change,' Martinet posited that complex structural systems tend to change in line with a general process of simplification. Hence, the phonemic opposition between short and long vowels, which produced a relatively large inventory of vocalic phonemes in Latin, was 'economized' in the emerging phonemic systems of the Romance languages.

This is not unique to the Romance languages. In English, the so-called *great vowel shift* provides further evidence in support of Martinet's theory. This shift, which occurred during the fifteenth and sixteenth centuries, affected the pronunciation of all English long vowels. In Middle English, spoken from 1100 to 1500, the word *house* was pronounced with the vowel sound of the modern English word *boot*, while *boot* was pronounced with the vowel sound of the modern English *boat*. The change that affected the pronunciation of *house* also affected the vowels of *mouse*, *louse*, and *mouth*.

Another principle that has become widely accepted is the one put forward originally by the neogrammarians, namely, that sound change is regular. The comparative method is, in fact, implanted on this principle. Comparativists examine root words from different languages to see if they are similar enough to have once been the same word in a common ancestor language. By establishing that the sound differences between similar root words are the result of regular sound changes that occurred in the languages, they can support the conclusion that the different languages descended from the same original language. For example, by comparing the Latin word *pater* with its English translation, *father*, comparativists would claim that the two languages are genetically related because of certain similarities between the two words. They would then hypothesize that the Latin /p/ had changed to /f/ in English, and that the two words descended from the same original word. They would search for other examples to strengthen this hypothesis, such as the Latin word *piscis* and its English translation, *fish*, and the Latin *pes* and the English translation, *foot*. The sound change that relates /f/ in the Germanic languages to /p/ in most other branches of Indo-European is, actually, a famous sound change, part of the so-called *Grimm's law*, named after the great German neogrammarian Jakob Grimm.

Morphological Change

The morphological system of a language is also susceptible to change. An ongoing morphological change in English, for example, is the loss of the distinction between the nominative, or subject, form *who* and the accusative, or object, form *whom*. English speakers use both the *who* and *whom* forms for the object of a sentence, saying both 'Who did you see?' and 'Whom did you see?'

The Latin morphological system underwent a massive restructuring in its gradual evolution into Italian. This was a consequence of the many phonological changes that had taken place.

In effect, with final consonants being lost, and changes in the vowel system, Italian and the other neo-Latin dialects were faced with a morphological system in disarray. Take, for example, Latin noun morphology. Latin nouns were declined in predictable ways. For instance, the first-declension feminine noun PUELLA (girl) was declined as follows:

Nominative	PUELLA *girl*	PUELLAE *girls*
Genitive	PUELLAE *of the girl*	PUELLARUM *of the girls*
Dative	PUELLAE *to the girl*	PUELLIS *to the girls*
Accusative	PUELLAM *the girl*	PUELLAS *the girls*
Ablative	PUELLA *from the girl*	PUELLIS *from the girls*
Vocative	PUELLA *Oh girl!*	PUELLAE *Oh girls!*

Now, as a consequence of phonological changes, the suffix morphemes that indicated case function were lost. As a result, new grammatical devices were introduced in the Romance languages to maintain case distinctions: for example, the preposition *a* became necessary to distinguish dative from accusative:

Ho telefonato alla ragazza   (= dative = indirect object)
Ho chiamato la ragazza   (= accusative = direct object).

Articles and other determiner structures, too, were adopted by the Romance languages to carry the load of various other case structure relations. Morphological change is a concomitant of sound change. Although this comes under various names in the linguistic literature, it can be called the principle of the *historical cycle*, to emphasize the fact that change in form and function is connected cyclically to change in sound.

Syntactic Change

As we discussed briefly in Chapter 1, as a result of morphological changes, the word order in an Italian sentence took on much more importance than it had in Latin, assuming, in effect, the functions of inflections, declensions, cases, and the like. In Latin the sentence *The boy* (PUER) *loves* (AMAT) *the girl* (PUELLAM) could have been rendered in any one of six ways, as we saw, because the suffix morpheme on each word revealed what relation each had to the others: PUER is in the nominative case and is thus the subject of the sentence; PUELLAM is in the accusative case (nominative = PUELLA) and thus will always be interpreted as the object, no matter where it occurs in the sentence. In Italian, on the other hand, word order and the use of determiners took over the function of the cases. This is why the sentences *Il ragazzo ama la ragazza* and *La ragazza ama il ragazzo* produce different meanings. Once again, the principle of the historical cycle can be seen to operate at this level as well. The cycle can be shown schematically as follows:

phonological change → morphological change → syntactic change

Semantic and Lexical Change

As we have discussed several times previously, the meanings of words can also change. In Middle English, the word *nice* usually had the meaning 'foolish,' and sometimes 'shy,' but never the modern meaning of 'pleasant.' Words can not only change their meaning but also become obsolete, and thus become discarded. For example, the word *uscio* for *porta* is virtually never used in Italian any longer, even in Tuscany where it originated.

While much change takes place in a given language without outside interference, many lexical changes can result from contact with other languages. As we have seen in this and other chapters, the most common cases of borrowing are lexical.

Borrowing can affect not only vocabulary but also, in principle, all components of a language's grammar. The English suffix /-er/, which is added to verbs to form nouns, as in the formation of *baker* from *bake*, is ultimately a borrowing from the Latin suffix /-arius/. The suffix has been incorporated to such an extent, however, that it is used with indigenous words, such as *bake*, as well as with Latin words. Although in principle any component of language can be borrowed, some components are much more susceptible to borrowing than others. Cultural vocabulary is the most susceptible to borrowing, while morphology is the least susceptible.

Concluding Remarks

We conclude this chapter and this book by reiterating one last time what we have said throughout, namely that language is an organism whose vital parts can be studied systematically with the diagnostic tools made available by the science of linguistics. Our final thought is, however, cautionary. No matter how scientific or theoretically sound a linguist's account of language might appear, no science can ever truly account for the remarkable phenomenon that we call language. We might be able to describe what the bits and pieces are like and how they hold together, but we will never be able to put into a theory or model all there is to know about language.

In a sense, linguistic analysis is comparable to solving a jigsaw puzzle. The goal of the puzzle solver is to figure out how the pieces of the puzzle fit together to produce the hidden picture that they conceal as disconnected pieces. But solving the jigsaw puzzle tells the solver nothing about why she is fascinated by such puzzles in the first place, nor what relevance they have to human life. Analogously, the linguist seeks to figure out how the bits and pieces (phonemes, morphemes, etc.) cohere into the organism of language. But having described the anatomy and physiology of this organism, he or she is still left with the dilemma of why people communicate verbally, why narratives, poems, and plays are so intrinsic to human life, and what relevance speech has, if any, to human survival.

Follow-Up Activities

1. Define the following terms and notions in your own words.

   calque
   pidgin

creole
sociolect
slang
argot
jargon
pubilect

2. What effect does speaking a geographical dialect have on speaking the standard language?

3. How would a native northern Italian speaker tend to pronounce the following words?

bello
tutto
a casa
davvero
soprattutto
tappo
buttare
occhio
nonno

4. How would a native speaker of Neapolitan pronounce the following words?

aspettare
sbaglio
stupido
sfera
scuola
snello
slittare
svendita

5. Why is the Italian spoken in immigrant communities so laden with loanwords and calques?

6. Explain the linguistic processes that underlie the nativization of

the following loanwords found commonly in the Italian spoken in the United States and Canada.
Example: garbiccio
This form shows: (1) addition of the final /-o/, thus assigning it to the masculine gender; (2) the doubling of the intervocalic consonant.

basamento (basement)
fornace (furnace)
sciabola (shovel)
naisse (nice)
floro (floor)
silingo (ceiling)
sinco (sink)
draivare (to drive)
squisare (to squeeze)

7. Explain the difference between a pidgin and a creole language.

8. Explain the difference among slang, argot, jargon, and pubilect.

9. List and discuss any emotive language mannerisms of current teen pubilect that you might know.

10. List and discuss any connotative language mannerisms of current teen pubilect that you might know.

11. Discuss the theory of sound change put forward by André Martinet. Can you give any examples of economically motivated changes in Italian?

12. Give examples of regular sound change in the development of Italian from Latin.

13. Explain the principle called the historical cycle in this chapter.

14. Explain the role of borrowing in linguistic change.

Glossary of Technical Terms

acoustic phonetics   study of the pattern of sound waves produced by vocal sounds and how they are perceived by the ear.

addition rule   rule that adds an element to a word, syllable, etc.

addressee   initiator of discourse.

addresser   intended receiver of discourse.

affix   morpheme that is added to another morpheme.

allomorph   variant of a morpheme – the actual form that a morpheme takes in a phrase. For example, /un/, /uno/, and /una/ are all allomorphs of the same indefinite article morpheme.

allophone   variant of a phoneme – the actual form that a phoneme takes in a word. For example, the [s] and [z] sounds are allophones of /s/: the voiced one, [z], occurs before another voiced consonant (*sbaglio*) and between vowels (*casa*); the latter occurs elsewhere (*specchio, segno,* etc.).

analytic language   language that depends mainly on word order to convey meaning.

anaphoric device   word or particle that refers back to a word uttered or written previously in a sentence or a discourse: e.g., <u>Alessandro</u> *dice che anche <u>lui</u> vuole venire al cinema con te.*

antonym   word with the opposite meaning of another word: e.g., *notte – giorno.*

argot   slang of specialized groups, especially criminals.

articulatory phonetics   description of the sounds of a language in terms of how they are articulated.

assimilation   process by which one sound in contact with another assumes one or all of its phonetic properties.

base rule   rule that specifies how a symbol in deep structure is expanded.

beat gesture   gesture accompanying speech by which the hand moves in such a way that it appears to keep beat.

binding   syntactic process by which certain forms are bound to each other.

borrowing   process of adopting a word from another language, for general use: e.g., Italian has borrowed the word *sport* from English.

bound morpheme   morpheme that must be attached to another morpheme in a phrase or sentence: e.g., the /il-/ in *illecito*.

calque   translation of a foreign syntactic structure: e.g., in Italiese *bassa città* translates *downtown* literally.

cataphoric device   word or particle that anticipates a word in a sentence or discourse: e.g., *È vero che ci vuole andare anche Sara in Italia?*

circumfix   two affixes that are added simultaneously to a morpheme.

closed syllable   syllable that ends in a consonant: e.g., the *con-* in *contare*.

coda   end part of a syllable.

code   system of signs such as language.

cohesive gesture   gesture accompanying speech that seems to tie the meanings in the discourse together imagistically.

communicative competence   ability to use a language appropriately in social context.

commutation test   comparing two forms that are alike in all respects except one in order to see if a difference in meaning results: e.g., *pane* vs. *cane*.

comparative method   method of comparing forms between languages to see if they are related.

complementary distribution   process whereby one form does not occur in the same environment as another.

complementary lengthening   process whereby the stressed vowel is lengthened in an open syllable before a single consonant.

conative function   effect a message has on its receiver.

conceptual metaphor   generalized metaphorical formula that underlies many single metaphors: e.g., [people are animals] underlies *He's a dog, She's a cat*, etc.

connotation   extensional meanings of a word.

consonant   sound produced with some obstruction to the air stream emanating from the lungs.

contact   the physical situation in which discourse occurs.

context   the psychological, social, and cultural relations people assume during discourse.

continuant   a sound produced through a nonstoppage of the air stream.

contour   the sound that can come before or after a nuclear vowel.

contrast (opposition)   the minimal difference between two elements.

creole   language that has been shaped by contact with other languages.

cultural model   connections among conceptual metaphors for delivering a certain concept.

deep structure   level of syntax where basic phrase structure is formed.

deictic gesture   gesture accompanying speech that attempts to locate the ideas in the discourse as occurring before or after.

deixis   process whereby something is pointed out as existing in some spatial, temporal, or relational form: e.g., *qui, su, prima*.

deletion rule   rule that deletes some element.

denotation   intentional meaning of a word.

derivational morpheme   morpheme that is derived from some other morpheme: e.g., *incautamente* is derived from *incauto*.

diachronic analysis   analysis of change in language.

dialect   regional or social version of a language.

dialect atlas   atlas that shows how the different dialectal forms are distributed geographically.

dialectology   study of dialects.

discourse   message constructed linguistically according to social context.

displacement   feature of language whereby a word evokes what it stands for even if it is not present for the senses to process.

distinctive feature   minimal trait in a form that serves to keep it distinct from other forms.

double consonant   a consonant that is longer or stronger than a simple one.

embedding   process of joining two or more sentences into one.

emotive function   speaker's intent during discourse.

feature-changing rule   rule that changes a feature in a form or sound.

figurative meaning   metaphorical meaning.

frame   discourse situation that is highly predictable.

free morpheme   morpheme that can exist on its own in a phrase: e.g., the *cauta* in *incautamente*.

free variation   existence of two variant forms: e.g., *tra* and *fra*.

gambit   verbal strategy for initiating or maintaining discourse flow.

generative syntax   analysis of language based on deriving the rules by which sentences are generated.

genetic classification   classification of languages by relating them to a source language.

gesture   communication involving hand movement.

gorgia toscana   phenomenon whereby intervocalic voiceless stops are aspirated; typical of Tuscany.

Gothic line   imaginary line running through La Spezia and Rimini which divides the Romance languages into Western (north of the line) and Eastern (south of the line).

government   syntactic process by which one category governs others in phrase structure.

grammar   system of structures that hold the morphological and syntactic systems together systematically.

grammatical morpheme   morpheme with grammatical meaning: e.g., *questo*.

ground   meaning of a metaphor

history of derivation   rules applied in the generation of a specific sentence.

holophrase   one-word utterance employed by children.

homograph   word that is spelled the same as another but with a different meaning: e.g., *porta* as in *Apri la porta* vs. *porta* in *Porta anche tua sorella*.

homonym   word that is pronounced or spelled the same as another but with a different meaning.

homophone   word that is pronounced the same as another but with a different meaning: *aunt – ant*.

hyponym   a word that is inclusive of another: *fiore* is a hyponym of *rosa*.

iconic gesture   gesture accompanying discourse that depicts a meaning through hand movement.

illocutionary act   type of speech act that specifies a call to action: e.g., *Vieni qui!*

infix   affix added internally to another morpheme: e.g., the /-isk/ in *capisco*.

inflection   change in the form of a word.

inflectional morpheme   morpheme that results from inflection.

intonation   pitch and tone in language.

irony   word or statement used in such a way that it means the opposite of what it denotes: *Che bella giornata!* uttered on a stormy day.

jargon   slang of specialized groups (e.g., lawyers, doctors, etc.).

language   system of verbal representation and communication.

langue   theoretical knowledge of language.

lenition   voicing of intervocalic plosives.

lexeme   morpheme with lexical meaning: e.g., the *logico* in *illogico*.

lexical field   collection of lexemes that are interrelated thematically (e.g., sports vocabulary).

lexical insertion   rule that inserts a lexeme into phrase structure.

lexicography   dictionary making.

lexicon   set of morphemes in a language.

linguistic competence   abstract knowledge of a language.

linguistic performance   knowledge of how to use a language.

linguistics   scientific study of language.

loanword   word borrowed from another language: e.g., *cifra* was borrowed from the Arabic language.

locutionary act   speech act that entails a referential statement: *La mia camicetta è verde.*

manner of articulation   how a sound is articulated.

marked category or form   category that is specific and not representative of the entire category.

message   information or intent of discourse.

metalingual function   referring to the forms of language used in discourse: *La parola nome è un nome.*

metaphony   effect of the final vowel on the stressed vowel.

metaphor   process by which something concrete is made to stand for something abstract: *Love is sweet.*

metaphoric gesture   gesture accompanying speech that represents the vehicle (concrete part) of a metaphor used in the discourse.

metonymy   process whereby the part stands for the whole: *la Casa Bianca* for "the American government."

minimal pair   pair like *pane – cane* in which the forms are the same except in one sound in the same position.

morpheme   minimal unit of meaning: e.g., in *incautamente* there are three morphemes: /in-/, /kauto/, and /-mente/.

morphology   level of language where words are formed.

name   word that identifies a person (and by extension animals, products, etc.).

narrative   story-like discourse.

nativization   process whereby a loanword is reshaped phonetically to become indistinguishable from a native word.

neo-Latin dialect   linguistic code derived from Latin.

noncontinuant   consonant that is produced through complete blockage of the air stream; e.g., [p], [t].

nonsegmental feature   feature that is not vocalic or consonantal.

nucleus   core of a syllable, usually a vowel

object   meaning of a word.

obstruent   sound produced with a degree of obstruction.

onomastics   study of names.

onset   part that precedes a nuclear vowel.

open syllable   syllable ending in a vowel.

palatalization   process by which a sound becomes a palatal.

parole   knowledge of how to use a language.

perlocutionary act   speech act that entails request for some action: e.g., *Mi può aiutare?*

phatic function   use of language to make or maintain social contact: e.g., *Come va?*

phoneme   minimal unit of sound that distinguishes meaning.

phonetics   description of how sounds are articulated.

phonological rule   rule that specifies how a phoneme is realized.

phonology   sound system of a language.

phrase structure   basic type of word arrangement in the construction of sentences.

pidgin   language that results from contact with a dominant language, taking its forms and simplifying them.

poetic function   language that aims to have an emotive effect.

point of articulation   place in the mouth where a sound is articulated.

pragmatics   study of discourse.

prefix   affix that is added before another morpheme: e.g., the /il-/ in *illogico*.

pubilect   teenage discourse

questione della lingua   historical question regarding the proper form of standard Italian.

redundant feature   feature that is predictable and thus not contrastive.

referent   what a word refers to.

referential function   use of language to refer to something other than the context in which it is uttered.

register   level of language in social situations.

repair   device for correcting misused language form.

rewrite rule   rule that expands a syntactic symbol.

Romance language   language descended from Latin.

root morpheme   morpheme with lexical meaning in a complex word: the form *logico* in *illogicamente*.

segmentation   decomposing a form or a phrase into its minimal elements: e.g., the word *illogicamente* can be segmented into *il-, logico,* and *-mente.*

semantics   study of meaning in language.

sentence   minimal syntactic unit.

sigmatic plural   pluralization of forms by adding the suffix /-s/.

sign   something that stands for something other than itself.

signification   meaning of a sign.

signified   what a sign refers to.

signifier   physical part of a sign.

simplification   rendering double consonants as single consonants.

slang   socially based variant of a language used by specific groups.

sociolect   social dialect.

sonorant   voiced sound.

source domain   concrete part of a conceptual metaphor: e.g., the [sweet] in [love is sweet].

speech act   specific use of language to imply an action.

stem morpheme   *See* root morpheme

stress   degree of force used to pronounce a vowel.

structuralism   type of linguistic analysis aiming to study language as a system of structures.

subcategorization   rule that classifies a lexeme according to its potential uses in syntax.

subject   noun phrase that is joined to the S-node in a sentence.

suffix   affix added to the end of a morpheme: e.g., the /-mente/ in *logicamente*.

suprasegmental feature   feature that is not vocalic or consonantal (e.g., tone).

surface structure   linear form that a sentence takes.

syllable   minimal breath group in the pronunciation of words.

synchronic analysis   study of language at a particular point in time, usually the present.

synonym   word that has the same (approximate) meaning as another word: *felice – contento*.

syntactic category   class of words that have the same function in syntax.

syntactic doubling   process whereby the initial consonant of a word is doubled when preceded by certain words ending in a vowel.

syntax   study of how sentences are organized.

synthetic language   highly inflectional language that does not depend on word order to deliver meaning.

target domain   topic of a conceptual metaphor: e.g., the [love] in [love is sweet].

topic   what the metaphor is about.

transform   string of words that has undergone a transformational process.

transformational rule   rule that transforms phrase structure sequences into surface structures.

typological classification   classifying languages according to type of grammatical system they have.

universal grammar   set of principles that define language and are purported to be present in the brain at birth.

unmarked category or form   default form in a class of forms.

variation   process whereby forms vary according to geography, social class, etc.

vehicle   concrete part of a metaphor.

vocalization   process by which a consonant is changed to a vowel.

voicing   process whereby a voiceless consonant is voiced.

volgare   language spoken by the people.

vowel   sound produced with no obstruction.

vulgar Latin   spoken Latin.

Italian–English Glossary

....

This glossary contains all the Italian words used in the textbook. Adjectives are given in their masculine singular forms, and verbs in their infinitive forms.

A

a	at, to
abilità	ability
abitare	to live, dwell
abito	suit, dress
acciaio	stainless steel
acclamato	acclaimed
acqua	water
acquisire	to acquire
acre	very sour, bitter
addurre	adduce
adesso	now
aiuola	flower-bed
aiuto	help
algebra	algebra
alitare	to breathe
allora	then, therefore
alto	tall
altolocato	highly placed
altro	other
amare	to love
ambiente	environment, ambiance
àmbito	context, environs, ambiance
americano	American
amica	female friend
amicizia	friendship

amico	(male) friend
ammiraglio	admiral
amore	love
ampio	broad, ample
anche	also, too, even
ancora	yet, again, still
andare	to go
angelo	angel
anguria	watermelon
animale	animal
anno	year
antipasto	hors d'oeuvres
apprendere	to learn
apprendimento	learning
appresso	after, nearby
apprezzare	to appreciate
appuntamento	appointment
aprire	to open
aquila	eagle
arancione	orange
arare	to till, plough
argomento	topic
aria	air
arrivare	to arrive
arrivederci	good-bye (familiar)
arrivederLa	good-bye (formal)
arte	art
arto	limb
ascesa	ascent
aspettare	to wait
attaccabrighe	troublemaker
attaccare	to initiate, attack
attacco	attack
attento	careful
atto	act, apt
attribuire	to attribute
attributo	attribute
autobus	bus
automobile	automobile
avanguardia	avant-garde
avanti	ahead
avere	to have
azzeccare	to make a bull's-eye
azzurro	blue

B

baciare	to kiss
bacio	kiss
baffi	moustache
bagno	bathroom
ballare	to dance
ballata	dance, ballade
bambino	child
banca	bank
basso	short
bastare	to be enough
battaglia	battle
becco	beak
belare	to bleat
bello	beautiful, handsome
bene	well
bere	to drink
bianco	white
biblioteca	library
bilinguismo	bilingualism
biologia	biology
bisogno	need
bisticcio	squabble
blu	dark blue
bocca	mouth
botta	hit, smack
braccio	arm
bravo	good
brillante	brilliant
brutto	ugly
bue	ox
buio	dark
buonanotte	good night
buonasera	good evening
buongiorno	good morning, good day
buono	good
busta	envelope

C

cadere	to fall
caffè	coffee
cagna	female dog

cagnolina	female puppy
cagnolino	male puppy
calcio	soccer
caldo	hot
calmo	calm
calza	stock
camicetta	blouse
camicia	shirt
camminare	to walk
cammino	chimney
cane	dog
canna	fishing pole
cantare	to sing
capacità	capacity
capelli	hair
capellone	long-haired man
capire	to understand
capitale	capital
capo	head
capostazione	station master
cappa	cape
cappello	hat
capriccio	whim
caramella	candy
carne	meat
caro	dear
carro	cart
carta	paper
cartone	carton
casa	house
casto	chaste
catena	chain
causa	cause
cautela	caution
cauto	cautious
cavallo	horse
celebre	famous
celeste	light blue
cena	dinner
cenno	nod, cue
cento	hundred
centrale	central
centrare	to centre

centro	downtown, centre
cercare	to look for, search
cerebrale	cerebral
cervello	brain
che	which, that, who
chi	who
chiamare	to call
chiamarsi	to be named
chiaro	clear
chiave	key
chiesa	church
chiesto	asked
chiosco	kiosk
ci	there, us
ciao	bye
cielo	sky
cifra	digit
cinema	movies, cinema
cinque	five
cintura	belt
ciò	thus, so
cioè	that is
circondare	to surround
città	city
ciurma	gang, crew
classico	classical
cocomero	watermelon
coda	tail, coda
codice	code
cogliere	to pick
cognitivo	cognitive
colle	hill
collegato	connected
collo	neck
come	like, as
cominciare	to begin
comprare	to buy
comunicare	to communicate
con	with
condannare	to condemn
condotto	conducted
conoscere	to know
conoscitivo	knowing

conscio	conscious
considerare	to consider
considerevolmente	considerably
contare	to count
contento	happy, content
contro	against
controllo	control
convalidare	to authenticate
corpo	body
correggere	to correct
correre	to run
correttezza	correctness
corretto	correct
corrotto	corrupt
corso	course
corto	low
cosa	thing
così	so, as, such
cosiddetto	so-called
costare	to cost
costituire	to constitute
cotto	cooked
credere	to believe
critico	critical
croce	cross
cucchiaio	spoon
cugina	female cousin
cugino	male cousin
cuoco	cook
cuore	heart
cupo	dark, low
cura	cure

D

da	from
d'accordo	OK
dare	to give
davanti	in front of
davvero	really
debordare	to overflow
decadere	to come down

definire	to define
deificare	to deify
delizia	delight
dente	tooth
dentro	inside
descrivere	to describe
desiderare	to desire
di	of
diametralmente	diametrically
diciotto	eighteen
di fronte	in front of
digerire	to digest
digiuno	empty stomach
dimostrare	to demonstrate, show
dire	to say
diritto	straight ahead
discorso	discourse, talk
discoteca	disco
discussione	discussion, argument
disdire	to undo, cancel
disfare	to undo
disfunzionalità	dysfunctionality
disgustare	to disgust
disperdere	to scatter
distante	distant
dito	finger
divenire	to become
diverso	diverse
diviso	divided
domani	tomorrow
dominante	dominant
donna	woman
dono	gift
dopo	after
dormire	to sleep
dote	dowry
dove	where
dovere	to have to
drastico	drastic
due	two
duomo	dome
duplicare	to duplicate
durante	during

E

e	and
ecco	here is, there is
educazione	good manners, training
elefante	elephant
elefantessa	female elephant
elettronico	electronic
epoca	epoch
era	era
ergastolo	life imprisonment
erroneo	erroneous
errore	error
esserci	to be there
essere	to be
essere simpatico a	to be pleasing to
età	age

F

fa	ago
faccia	face
facile	easy
facilità	facility
falce	sickle
falco	falcon
fallo	wrong (n.)
fame	hunger
famiglia	family
famoso	famous
fantasia	imagination
fare	to do
farmacia	pharmacy
fascia	band, tape
fato	fate
fatto	fact
favorire	to favour
fegato	liver
felice	happy
fenomeno	phenomenon
fermentare	to ferment
ferro	steel
fiamma	flame

fienile	haystack
fieno	hay
fierezza	pride
figlia	daughter
figlio	son
filo	string, thread
filosofia	philosophy
finalità	end, objective
fine	end
finestra	window
finire	to end, stop
finto	fake
fiore	flower
fisica	physics
fiume	river
fiumicino	stream
follia	madness
fondatezza	soundness
forma	form
formazione	background
forse	maybe
forte	strong
fortuna	fortune, luck
francese	French
frase	phrase
fratello	brother
freddezza	coldness
freddo	cold
fresco	fresh
frigo	refrigerator
fronte	forehead
fune	rope
funzionare	to function
fuori	outside
furbo	shrewd

G

gamba	leg
gatta	female cat
gatto	cat
gelato	ice cream
gelo	frost, iciness

geloso	jealous
generale	general
gente	people
geometrico	geometrical
gettare	to throw
ghetto	ghetto
già	already
giallo	yellow
giapponese	Japanese
ginocchio	knee
giocare	to play
giocatore	player
gioco	game
gioiello	jewel
giorno	day
giro	turn
giù	down
giubba	jacket
giugno	June
giurare	to swear
giustizia	justice
giusto	correct, right, just
glicerina	glycerin
globo	globe
gnocco	dumpling
godersi	to enjoy oneself
gola	throat
gomito	elbow
governo	government
grande	big
greco	Greek
grigio	grey
grosso	large, huge
guancia	cheek
guardare	to look at
guerra	war
guidare	to drive
gusto	taste, flavour

I

idea	idea
ieri	yesterday

illecito	illicit
illogico	illogical
illuminato	illuminated
imboccare	to spoonfeed
imbrogliare	to deceive
imitare	to imitate
impero	empire
impiccio	jam
impiego	job
importante	important
importanza	importance
impossibile	impossible
imprevedibile	unexpected
improbabile	improbable
in	in
incassare	to cash in
incautamente	uncautiously
inchiostro	ink
incomprensibile	incomprehensible
incongruo	incongruous
incontrare	to encounter, meet
incoraggiato	encouraged
incredibile	incredible
indagine	research, inquiry
indifendibile	indefensible
industria	industry
infanzia	infancy
infedeltà	infidelity
infermiera	nurse
infermiere	male nurse
inferno	hell
ingegno	ingenuity
inglese	English
ingrosso	wholesale
innamorato	in love
inno	anthem
insaputa	unbeknownst
insegnante	teacher
insieme	together
insincero	insincere
intelligente	intelligent
interferenza	interference
internazionale	international

intollerabile	intolerable
invece	instead
io	I
ira	anger
irregolare	irregular
irresponsabile	irresponsible
irrilevante	irrelevant
isola	island
isolato	city block
Italia	Italy
italiano	Italian
iugoslavo	Yugoslavian

L

labbro	lip
lago	lake
lampada	lamp
lasciare	to leave (behind)
lato	side
latta	tin
latte	milk
leccare	to lick
lecito	licit
legare	to tie
leggere	to read
lei	she
lettera	letter
lettore	reader
lezione	lesson
lì	there
libreria	bookstore
libro	book
lingua	language
linguistico	linguistic
lira	lira
livello	level
logico	logical
lontano	far
loro	they
luce	light
luglio	July
lui	he

luna	moon
lunedì	Monday
lungo	long
lusso	luxury

M

ma	but
macchina	car
madre	mother
magari	maybe
magazzino	department store
maglia	sweater
mai	ever
maiale	pig
mainare	to lower
male	bad
mamma	mom
mancare	to lack
mandare	to send
mangiare	to eat
mano	hand
mappa	map
mare	sea
marito	husband
marrone	brown
martedì	Tuesday
massimo	maximum
materia	subject
medioevale	medieval
mela	apple
melone	melon
memoria	memory
mentalità	mentality
mente	mind
mento	chin
mentre	while
menzionare	to mention
mese	month
mettere	to put
mezzo	half
mio	my
moda	style, fashion

modello	model
moderno	modern
moglie	wife
moltiplicato	multiplied
molto	a lot
mondo	world
montagna	mountain
mossa	move
mostrare	to show
moto	motorcycle, motion
mucca	cow
muro	wall
mutare	to change

N

nascita	birth
naso	nose
necessario	necessary
negare	to deny
negozio	store
nero	black
nessuno	no one
neve	snow
né ... né	neither ... nor
niente	nothing
no	no
noce	walnut
noi	we
nome	name
non	not
nonna	grandmother
nonno	grandfather
nono	ninth
nostro	our
notevole	notable
notte	night
nove	nine
nuotare	to swim
nuovo	new

O

o	or
oca	goose
occhio	eye
occidentale	western
odiare	to hate
oggi	today
ogni	every
oltre	other
opera	opera, work
opposto	opposite
ora	hour, now
orecchio	ear
origine	origin
oro	gold
orologio	watch
ortica	nettle grass
orto	garden
oscuro	obscure, dark
osso	bone
ottimo	outstanding
otto	eight

P

padella	pan
padre	father
padroneggiare	to command
pagare	to pay
palco	stage, platform
palcoscenico	theatre stage
palla	ball
panca	bench
pane	bread
pantaloni	pants
parallelo	parallel
parco	park
parere	to seem
parlare	to speak
parola	word

partenza	departure
particolarmente	particularly
partire	to leave, depart
partita	game, match
pasta	pasta
pasticcio	mess
pasto	meal
pattinare	to skate
patto	pact
paura	fear
pausa	pause
pausare	to pause
pazienza	patience
pelle	skin
penisola	peninsula
penna	pen
pensarci	to think about
pensare	to think
pensiero	thought
pentire	to regret
per	for, through
pera	pear
percezione	perception
perché	why, because
perdere	to lose
periodo	period
permettere	to permit, allow
pero	pear tree
persona	person
personale	personal
pesce	fish
peso	weight
petto	chest
pezzo	piece
piacere	to like
piatto	plate
piazza	town/city square
piccolo	small
piede	foot
pieno	full
pieno zeppo	really full
pino	pine
pista	path

più	more, plus
piuma	feather
pizza	pizza
plasticità	plasticity
plurilinguismo	plurilingualism
poco	few, little
poi	*then*
polemica	polemics
polso	pulse
pomeriggio	afternoon
porre	to put
porta	door
portalettere	letter carrier
porto	port
possedimento	possession
possibile	possible
posta	mail
posto	place
potenziale	potential
potere	to be able to
povero	poor
pozzo	puddle
pratico	practical
prato	field
precisione	precision
precludere	to preclude
predire	to predict
preferire	to prefer
prefigurazione	prefigurement
prendere	to take
preoccuparsi	to worry
presentire	to anticipate
presidente	president
prevedere	to foretell
prevedibile	likely
prima	before
primo	first
principale	principal
probabile	probable
produzione	production
professionale	professional
professore	professor
profondo	profound, deep

programma	program
promettere	to promise
proposito	matter, intent
proposto	proposed
psicologia	psychology
psicologico	psychological
psicologo	psychologist
pubblico	public
pubertà	puberty
puerile	puerile, childish
pungere	to pinch
punta	tip
punto	point
purgare	to expunge
puzzare	to smell

Q

quadro	painting
qualcuno	someone
quale	which
quando	when
quanto	how much
quasi	almost
quello	that
quello che	what, that which
questione	question, issue
questo	this
questura	police station
qui	here
quotidianamente	daily

R

ragazza	girl
ragazzo	boy
ragione	reason, right
raro	rare
razza	race
reazione	reaction
reciproco	reciprocal
regalo	gift
reggere	to hold

regione	region
regolare	to regulate
responsabile	responsible
rete	network
ricco	rich
ricerca	research
ricordare	to remember
rientrare	to fit in
rilevante	relevant
rilevare	to point out
rinfresco	refreshment
risorgere	to re-emerge
rispetto a	regarding, compared with
rivoluzione	revolution
roba	things
rosa	pink, rose
rosso	red
rossore	redness
rotto	broken
rovescio	reverse
rovinare	to ruin
ruolo	role
ruscello	stream, rivulet

S

sale	salt
salotto	living room
saltare	to jump
salutare	to greet
salute	health
sangue	blood
santo	saint
sapere	to know
sapienza	knowledge
sapore	taste, flavour
sbaglio	mistake
sborsare	to dish out
scarpa	shoe
scaturire	to arise
scemo	silly
scherzo	joke, prank
schiena	back

sciabola	sabre
sciare	to ski
scientifico	scientific
sciocco	bland
sciopero	labour strike
scolarizzazione	schooling
scolorire	to discolour
scolpire	to sculpt
sconfitta	defeat
scopa	broom
scopo	goal
scoprire	to discover
scorso	last (as in 'last year')
scrivere	to write
scuola	school
scusa	excuse me
sdraiarsi	to lie down
se	if
secchio	pail
secco	dry
secolo	century
secondo	second, according to
sedia	chair
semiotica	semiotics
sempre	always
sensibile	sensitive
sentire	to hear
sentirsi	to feel
sera	evening
serpe	snake
serra	greenhouse
settimana	week
settimo	seventh
sfera	sphere
si	oneself
sì	yes
sia ... che	both ... and
signora	madam, Mrs, Ms
signore	sir, Mr.
simpatico	nice
simultaneo	simultaneous
singolo	single
slittare	to slide

smettere	to stop
snello	slim
società	society
sofà	sofa
soffiare	to blow
sogno	dream
sonno	sleep
soprano	soprano
soprattutto	above all else
sopravvivenza	survival
sorella	sister
sospiro	sigh
spada	sword
spagnolo	Spanish
spalla	shoulder
sparare	to shoot
specchio	mirror
spedire	to send, mail
spendere	to spend
speranza	hope
sperare	to hope
spesa	shopping
spiegare	to explain
spirito	spirit
sprecare	to waste
spreco	waste
squadra	team
stanco	tired
stare	to stay
stendere	to lay out
stesso	the same
stilista	designer
stivale	boot
strada	road
studente	student
studentessa	female student
studio	study
stufo	fed up
stupido	stupid
stupire	to amaze
su	up
successo	success
summenzionato	above-mentioned

sunto	gist, summary
suo	his/her
suono	sound
superficiale	superficial, surface
svelare	to unveil
svendita	sale
sviluppo	development
svolgere	to unfold

T

tacco	heel
tale	such
tana	den
tangenziale	tangential
tanto	much
tappo	cork
tattica	tactic
tatto	tact
tavolo	table
tè	tea
teatro	theatre
tedesco	German
telefonare	to phone
televisione	television
tempo	time, weather
tenere	to keep
tenore	tenor
teoria	theory
terra	earth
terzo	third
tesi	thesis
testa	head
tetto	roof
tollerabile	tolerable
topo	mouse
tornare	to return
toro	bull
torre	tower
tosse	cough
tra	between, among
treno	train
triste	sad

troppo	too much
trovare	to find
tu	you
tulipano	tulip
tuo	your
turista	tourist
tutti	everyone
tutto	all

U

ultimo	last
unghia	fingernail
uomo	man
urto	smash, hit
uscire	to go out
uso	use
uva	grapes

V

valore	worth, value
vano	vain
vasto	vast
vecchio	old
vedere	to see
veloce	fast
velocità	velocity, speed
vendere	to sell
venire	to come
venti	twenty
ventiduesimo	twenty-second
ventinovesimo	twenty-ninth
ventitreesimo	twenty-third
vento	wind
ventottesimo	twenty-eighth
veramente	truly, really
verde	green
verità	truth
vero	true
verosimile	realistic
verosimilitudine	verisimilitude
verso	towards

vettura	vehicle
via	way
vicino	near
vigliacco	coward
vincente	winning
vincere	to win
vincita	win, victory
vino	wine
viola	purple
vita	life
vitto	food
vittoria	victory
vivere	to live
voga	vogue
voi	you
volentieri	gladly
volere	to want
volgo	common people
volpe	fox
vorace	voracious
vostro	yours
vuoto	empty

X

xenofobia	xenophobia

Z

zero	zero
zio	uncle
zitto	quiet
zucchero	sugar
zuppa	soup

Further Reading

The following are suggestions for further reading on the topics touched upon in each chapter. The selection below is not a comprehensive list. It has been put together simply to provide a minimal reading list that we believe will allow the interested reader to fill in many of the gaps left by our treatments.

Chapter 1

Auerbach, E. *Lingua letteraria e pubblico nella tarda antichità latina e nel Medioevo.* Milano: Feltrinelli, 1960.

Dardano, M. *G. I. Ascoli e la questione della lingua.* Roma: Istituto dell'Enciclopedia Italiana, 1974.

De Mauro, T. *Storia linguistica dell'Italia unita.* Bari: Laterza, 1976.

Devoto, G. *Il linguaggio d'Italia. Storia e strutture linguistiche italiane dalla preistoria ai nostri giorni.* Milano: Rizzoli, 1974.

Elcock, D. *The Romance Languages.* London: Faber, 1960.

Gensini, S. *Elementi di storia linguistica italiana.* Bergamo: Minerva Italica, 1990.

Grassi, C. *Elementi di dialettologia italiana.* Torino: G. Giappichelli, 1970.

Lepschy, A.L., and G. Lepschy. *La lingua italiana. Storia, varietà dell'uso, grammatica.* Milano: Bompiani, 1981.

Migliorini, B. *Storia della lingua italiana.* Firenze: Sansoni, 1960.

Pei, M.A. *The Italian Language.* New York: Columbia University Press, 1941.

Tagliavini, C. *Le origini delle lingue neolatine.* Bologna: Pàtron, 1972.

Vitale, M. *La questione della lingua.* Palermo: Palumbo, 1960.

Zolli, P. *Le parole straniere.* Bologna: Zanichelli, 1976.

Chapter 2

Fromkin, V., and R. Rodman. *An Introduction to Language*, 6th ed. New York: Harcourt Brace, 1998.

Robins, R.H.A. *A Short History of Linguistics*, 3rd ed. London: Longman, 1990.

Saussure, F. de. *Cours de linguistique générale*. Paris: Payot, 1916.

Chapter 3

Ladefoged, P.A. *A Course in Phonetics*, 2nd ed. New York: Harcourt, Brace, Jovanovich, 1982.

Pullum, G., and W.A. Laudusaw. *Phonetic Symbol Guide*. Chicago: University of Chicago Press, 1986.

Chapter 4

Agard, F.B., and R.J. Di Pietro. *The Sounds of English and Italian*. Chicago: University of Chicago Press, 1965.

Brakel, A. *Phonological Markedness and Distinctive Features*. Bloomington: Indiana University Press. 1983.

Katamba, F. *An Introduction to Phonology*. London: Longman, 1989.

Kaye, J. *Phonology: A Cognitive View*. Hillsdale, NJ: Lawrence Erlbaum, 1989.

Lepschy, G.C. *Saggi di linguistica italiana*. Bologna: Il Mulino, 1978.

Muljačić, Z. *Fonologia della lingua italiana*. Bologna: Il Mulino, 1972.

Chapter 5

Agard, F.B., and R.J. Di Pietro. *The Grammatical Structures of English and Italian*. Chicago: University of Chicago Press, 1965.

Bauer, L. *Introducing English Morphology*. Edinburgh: Edinburgh University Press, 1988.

Hall, R.A. *Le strutture dell'italiano*. Roma: Armando, 1971.

Matthews, P.H. *Morphology: An Introduction to the Theory of Word-Structure*. Cambridge: Cambridge University Press, 1974.

Spencer, A. *Morphological Theory*. Oxford: Blackwell, 1991.

Chapter 6

Borsley, R.D. *Syntactic Theory: A Unified Approach*. Kent: Edward Arnold, 1991.

Haegeman, L. *An Introduction to Government and Binding Theory*. Oxford: Blackwell, 1991.

Langacker, R.W. *Concept, Image, and Symbol: The Cognitive Basis of Grammar*. Berlin: Mouton de Gruyter, 1990.

Lyons, J. *Chomsky*, 2nd ed. London: Fontana, 1991.

Radford, A. *Italian Syntax: Transformational and Relational Grammar.* Cambridge: Cambridge University Press, 1977.

– *Transformational Grammar: A First Course.* Cambridge: Cambridge University Press, 1988.

Smith, N. *The Twitter Machine: Reflections on Language.* Oxford: Blackwell, 1989.

Chapter 7

Allan, K. *Linguistic Meaning.* London: Routledge, 1986.

Chierchia, G., and S. McConnell-Ginet. *Meaning and Grammar.* Cambridge, MA: MIT Press, 1990.

Fucilla, J.G. *Our Italian Surnames.* Evanston, IL: Chandler's, 1943.

Gibbs, R.W. *The Poetics of Mind: Figurative Thought, Language, and Understanding.* Cambridge: Cambridge University Press, 1994.

Lakoff, G. *Women, Fire and Dangerous Things: What Categories Reveal about the Mind.* Chicago: University of Chicago Press, 1987.

Lakoff, G., and L. Johnson. *Metaphors We Live By.* Chicago: Chicago University Press, 1980.

Lakoff, G., and M. Turner. *More Than Cool Reason: A Field Guide to Poetic Metaphor.* Chicago: University of Chicago Press, 1989.

Nuessel, F. *The Study of Names: A Guide to the Principles and Topics.* Westport: Greenwood, 1992.

Taylor, J.R. *Linguistic Categorization: Prototypes in Linguistic Theory.* Oxford: Clarendon, 1989.

Chapter 8

Brown, G., and G. Yule. *Discourse Analysis.* Cambridge: Cambridge University Press, 1983.

Brown, P., and S.C. Levinson. *Politeness: Some Universals in Language Usage.* Cambridge: Cambridge University Press, 1987.

Halliday, M.A.K. *Introduction to Functional Grammar.* London: Arnold, 1985.

Joos, M. *The Five Clocks.* New York: Harcourt, Brace and World, 1967.

McNeill, D. *Hand and Mind: What Gestures Reveal about Thought.* Chicago: University of Chicago Press, 1992.

Morris, D. *Gestures: Their Origins and Distributions.* London: Cape, 1979.

Propp. V.J. *Morphology of the Folktale.* Austin: University of Texas Press, 1928.

Saville-Troike, M. *The Ethnography of Communication: An Introduction,* 2nd ed. Oxford: Blackwell, 1989.

Wardhaugh, R. *How Conversation Works.* Oxford: Blackwell, 1985.

Chapter 9

Anttila, R. *Historical and Comparative Linguistics,* 2nd ed. Amsterdam: John Benjamins, 1989.

Berruto, G. *La sociolinguistica.* Bologna: Zanichelli, 1974.

– *L'italiano impopolare.* Napoli: Guida, 1978.

Coates, J. *Women, Men and Language.* London: Longman, 1986.

Cortelazzo, M. *Avviamento critico allo studio della dialettologia italiana.* Pisa: Pacini, 1969/1972.

Danesi, M. *Cool: The Signs and Meanings of Adolescence.* Toronto: University of Toronto Press, 1984.

De Mauro, T., and M. Lodi. *Lingua e dialetti.* Roma: Editori Riuniti, 1979.

Downes, W.D. *Language and Society.* London: Fontana, 1983.

Haller, H. *Una lingua perduta e ritrovata. L'italiano degli italo-americani.* Firenze: La Nuova Italia, 1993.

– *The Other Italy: Literary Canon in Dialect.* Toronto: University of Toronto Press, 1999.

Holm, J.A. *Pidgins and Creoles.* Cambridge: Cambridge University Press, 1988/1989.

Maiden, M., and M. Parry, eds. *The Dialects of Italy.* London: Routledge, 1997.

Milroy, L. *Analyzing Linguistic Variation.* Oxford: Blackwell, 1987.

Sabatini, A. *Il sessismo nella lingua italiana.* Rome: Presidenza del Consiglio dei Ministri, 1987.

Tekavčič, P. *Grammatica storica della lingua italiana.* Bologna: Il Mulino, 1980.

Index